Usborne
Junior
Illustrated
SCIENCE
Dictionary

Usborne Quicklinks

The Usborne Quicklinks Website is packed with thousands of links to the best websites on the internet. The websites include information, video clips, sounds, games and animations that support and enhance the information in Usborne internet-linked books.

To visit the recommended websites for the Junior Illustrated Science Dictionary, go to the Usborne Quicklinks Website at www.usborne.com/quicklinks and enter the keywords: junior science

Internet safety

When using the internet please follow the internet safety guidelines displayed on the Usborne Quicklinks Website. The websites recommended in Usborne Quicklinks are regularly reviewed. However, the content of a website may change at any time and Usborne Publishing is not responsible for the content of websites other than its own. We recommend that children are supervised while on the internet.

Usborne
Junior
Illustrated
SCIENCE
Dictionary

Sarah Khan
and Dr. Lisa Jane Gillespie

Designed by
Michael Hill and Joanne Kirkby

Edited by Kirsteen Rogers

Illustrated by Lizzie Barber

Science education consultant:
Helen Wilson MEd, BSc (hons), PGCE
Oxford Brookes University

What is science?

Science is about asking big questions and thinking of big ideas about how the world works. You can use science to investigate your ideas in an organized way, and use the results of these investigations to see whether your ideas are right.

This book divides science into six main sections. If you'd like to find out about a whole subject, you can turn to the section or pages and read straight through. If you just want to look up a particular word or fact, use the index at the back of the book.

Living things

Explores what plants, animals and people need to live and grow healthily; and how the many different living things relate to each other and their environment

Materials

Describes different substances, what they are like, how they behave and how they can change

Forces

Explains how forces act on objects, the different types of forces, and how they can be used

Energy

Describes what energy is, where it is found, and how it is used in everyday life

The Earth and space

Explores space, including the stars, planets and black holes, and the Earth's relationship with the Sun and Moon

Science at work

Explains how to do science: how scientists think, do experiments and make sense of evidence, and introduces some famous scientists and their ideas

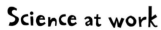

Contents

Life processes

There are seven activities that all living things do. These are called life processes. If something carries out all seven life processes, you know it's alive.

Movement

Living things move, changing their position by themselves. Most animals can move from place to place, which helps them find food or escape danger.

1. The cheetah is chasing its dinner.   **2.** The gazelle is running for its life.

A plant's own movements are very small or slow so they are much harder to see. Plants grow towards sunlight, slowly changing their position.

Some plants, such as sunflowers, turn during the day to follow the Sun as it moves across the sky.

Nutrition

Nutrition is the way living things get energy from chemicals called **nutrients.**

Most plants get nutrients from food they make inside their leaves.

Animals take in nutrients by eating plants or other animals.

Animals eat to get nutrients, but most plants make their own food. They use energy from sunlight to turn carbon dioxide gas and water into sugar and oxygen gas.

Respiration

All living things release energy from food by a process called respiration. Most of them need oxygen to do this.

Plants make a lot of their own oxygen. They also absorb it from the air through tiny holes in their leaves.

Many animals get the oxygen they need by breathing air into their lungs.

Fish use gills to absorb oxygen from water.

 Find out more about: **gravity** (pages 72-73); **movement** (pages 20-23); **nutrition** (pages 28-29); **reproduction** (pages 36-37); **senses** (pages 24-25)

Excretion

Excretion is the way living things get rid of waste substances that are left over after nutrition and respiration. Some waste is removed in faeces (poo); other substances are excreted in urine (wee) or breathed out as carbon dioxide gas.

Trees release oxygen, and get rid of waste substances inside their dead leaves when they fall off.

Autumn leaves contain waste substances.

Organisms

An organism is another name for a living thing.

Reproduction

All living things reproduce, which means they make new living things. If they didn't, their species would die out. For example, people have babies, cats have kittens, and most plants produce seeds as a way of making new plants.

Most plants make seeds that grow into new plants.

Animals produce young that grow into adults.

Growth

Growth means getting bigger. Some living things grow to a certain size, then stop. Others carry on growing for their whole lives.

Trees could keep on growing, given the right conditions.

This baby elephant will stop growing once it has become an adult.

Sensitivity

All living things are sensitive, which means they respond to the world around them. For example, people find out about their surroundings using their senses of sight, hearing, touch, taste and smell.

All plants are sensitive to light, water and gravity, and some can sense touch.

Venus flytraps spring shut when their sensitive hairs are touched.

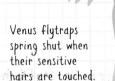

One way to remember the seven life processes is **Mrs. N-er-G** ("energy"):
Movement, Respiration, Sensitivity, Nutrition, Excretion, Reproduction, Growth

Living and non-living things

Everything is either living or non-living. Living things perform all seven life processes; non-living things don't. To decide if something is living or not, make a checklist of the life processes. If you can answer "yes" to every category, it's alive.

Cat

Movement	✓	It walks, runs and climbs
Respiration	✓	It breathes
Sensitivity	✓	It senses its surroundings
Nutrition	✓	It eats cat food and mice
Excretion	✓	It wees, poos and breathes out
Reproduction	✓	It gives birth to kittens
Growth	✓	It grows from a kitten into an adult cat

The cat does all of the seven life processes, so it's a living thing.

Car

Movement	?	It moves, but not by itself
Respiration	✓	It uses up oxygen
Sensitivity	?	It responds to the steering wheel
Nutrition	✓	It needs fuel
Excretion	✓	It gives off exhaust
Reproduction	✗	
Growth	✗	

The car only does some of the seven life processes, so it is non-living.

Cells

Living things are made up of tiny, living parts called cells, which are so small you need a microscope to see them. Some things are made of just one cell, and others contain millions. Knowing about cells can help you decide what's alive and what isn't.

Oak

Movement	✓	Its roots grow towards water
Respiration	✓	It uses oxygen to release energy from its food
Sensitivity	✓	It senses light
Nutrition	✓	It makes food using sunlight
Excretion	✓	It gives out gases and water
Reproduction	✓	It produces acorns
Growth	✓	It grows from an acorn into a tree
Cells	✓	

An oak has cells and does all the life processes, so it's living.

Flame

Movement	✓	It flickers and dances
Respiration	✓	It uses up oxygen
Sensitivity	?	It moves in a breeze
Nutrition	✓	It needs fuel
Excretion	✓	It gives off smoke
Reproduction	✓	It can start other fires
Growth	✓	It can grow and spread
Cells	✗	

A flame performs many of the life processes, but it isn't made up of living cells, so it's not living.

Find out more about: **life processes** (pages 6-7); **lungs** (page 33)
To help you remember about cells, you could give Mrs. NerG an initial: MRS. **C.** NERG

Once alive and never alive

Non-living things can be things that were once alive and are now made up of dead cells. Or they can be things that have never been alive, which are not made up of cells at all.

This jug and glass are not made up of cells because they were never alive.

The wood in this stool was once part of a living tree, and so is made up of cells.

Non-living parts

Organisms can be made up of dead as well as living cells – your hair's roots are alive, but the hair above the skin is dead. Some body parts were never alive, for example, shells.

Animal horns and hooves are non-living parts made up of cells that were once alive.

A snail's shell is a non-living part, but it is not made up of cells, so was never alive.

Cells, tissues and organs

Animals (including people) are made up of animal cells. Trees and flowers are made up of plant cells. Different types of animal and plant cells have different jobs to do.

A cell's shape and size depends on its job. Most cells can only be seen through a microscope.

Around 1,800 animal cells would fit onto this microscopic dot.

1. Cells that are of the same type join together into sheets called **tissues.**

Muscle cells are thin and stretchy.

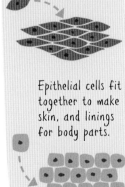

Epithelial cells fit together to make skin, and linings for body parts.

2. Different types of tissue join together to make **organs** that do particular jobs.

Organ (stomach)

Organ (small intestine)

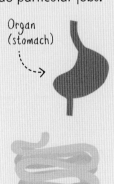

3. Organs combine to make **systems**; such as the circulatory or digestive system.

Digestive system

Large intestine (organ)

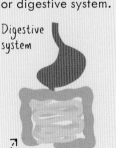

4. Different systems together make up a whole **organism**; a human is one kind.

Circulatory system

Find out more about: **human eggs** (page 36); **circulatory system** (page 32)

Looking at plants

Plants are living things that use energy from sunlight to make food. There are many different kinds — flowers, trees and grasses are all plants.

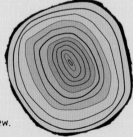

Parts of a plant

Most plants are made up of stems, flowers, leaves and roots. Each part has its own job to do to help the plant grow, stay healthy and make new plants.

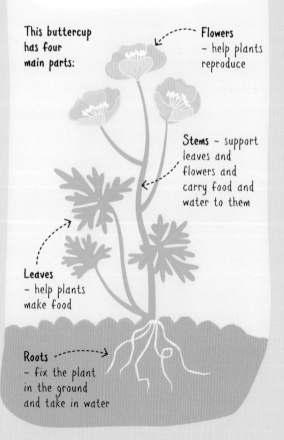

This buttercup has four main parts:

Flowers
- help plants reproduce

Stems - support leaves and flowers and carry food and water to them

Leaves
- help plants make food

Roots
- fix the plant in the ground and take in water

Roots

Roots anchor a plant in the ground and take in water from the soil.

Tiny hairs on the roots absorb water, minerals and oxygen from the soil into the plant.

There are two main kinds of roots:

Tap roots have one larger root, with smaller ones coming off it. Carrots are swollen tap roots.

Fibrous roots are all a similar size and spread out in all directions. Many grasses have fibrous roots.

Stems and trunks

Stems support leaves and flowers, helping them grow towards the sunlight. Stems also have tubes inside them which carry water and nutrients to all the different parts of the plant.

A tree's stem is its trunk. The tubes inside a tree trunk join up to form rings. A new ring grows every year.

This tree trunk has been cut across so you can see inside it. The number and thickness of its rings can tell you how long it lived and how well it grew.

Leaves

A plant's leaves are where it makes food and excretes waste. Tiny holes in the leaves' undersides excrete oxygen and let in carbon dioxide for making nutrients.

A green chemical called **chlorophyll** inside leaves uses sunlight energy to make food. In autumn, most plants stop making food. The chlorophyll breaks down to reveal other colours.

Green chlorophyll fades to show the colours of the sugars and the waste stored in the leaves.

Photosynthesis

Photosynthesis is the way a plant makes food. A plant uses energy from sunlight to turn water from the ground and carbon dioxide gas from the air into sugar and starch. This also produces oxygen gas.

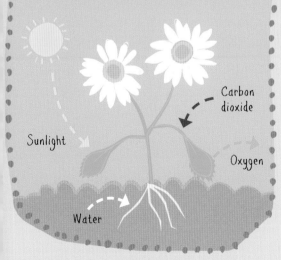

Sunlight

Carbon dioxide

Oxygen

Water

Flowers

Flowers contain a plant's reproductive organs. These are the parts that help a plant reproduce. There's more about flowers on pages 12–13.

Flowering plants

Flowering plants grow flowers to help them reproduce. There are over a quarter of a million kinds.

Non-flowering plants

Non-flowering plants don't grow flowers but reproduce in other ways:

• **Spores** – tiny reproductive cells that form on the leaves and drop to the ground to grow into a new plant.

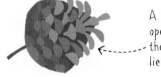

The brown dots on the underside of this fern leaf are full of spores.

• **Cones** – hard cases of overlapping scales produced by some trees, which contain seeds.

A cone's scales open to release the seeds that lie underneath.

• **Vegetative propagation** – new plants grow directly from a parent plant's leaf, stem or root. The new plant is exactly the same as its parent.

Strawberries reproduce by sending out stems from which new plants grow.

Find out more about: **carbon dioxide** (page 64); **excretion** (page 7); **nutrients** (page 6)

Looking at flowers

Flowers help plants reproduce. They are made up of different parts, and each part has its own job to do.

Parts of a flower

Most flowers are made up of several parts, such as petals, sepals, a carpel, and stamens. Not every type of flower contains all these parts, though.

The parts of a cherry blossom flower

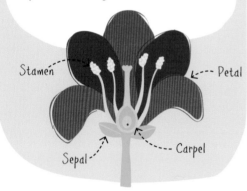

Stamen

Petal

Sepal

Carpel

Petals

Petals are the outer parts of a flower. They usually grow in a ring around the plant's reproductive organs, and are often bright and colourful.

A rock rose has five separate petals that form a flat ring around the middle of the flower.

A bluebell's five petals join to form a protective hood over its reproductive organs.

Flower buds and sepals

A flower bud is a newly formed flower made up of overlapping petals, protected by leaves called sepals. As the flower grows, the petals unfold and the sepals remain in a ring under the petals or wither and fall off.

Unopened petals

Sepal

Sepals and buds often grow from the tip of a plant's stem.

Stamens and carpels

A stamen is a flower's male organ. It has a stalk, called a **filament**, and a head, called an **anther**, which contains male sex cells called **pollen**.

Stamens are usually long and thin.

Anther

Filament

Pollen

A carpel is a flower's female organ. It has a stalk called a **style**, a sticky tip called a **stigma**, and a base housing an **ovary**. Here, female sex cells, called **eggs**, are made inside structures called **ovules**.

A flower's carpel is often shorter than its stamens.

Stigma

Style

Ovary

Ovule

Pollination

Pollination is the way pollen gets from a stamen to a stigma. There are two main types of pollination: insect and wind pollination.

Insect pollination

Insect pollination is when, during an insect's feeding visits to flowers, pollen from a stamen sticks to its body and is then rubbed onto a stigma.

Insects are attracted to scented flowers with bright petals, that produce a sweet liquid called nectar.

Bees and other insects transport pollen from flower to flower.

Wind pollination

Wind pollination is when the wind blows pollen from a stamen to a stigma. Most wind-pollinated flowers have dangling stamens that release clouds of pollen light enough to float on the breeze.

Crack willow flowers have stamens that release pollen when shaken by the wind.

Fertilization

Once a plant has been pollinated, its pollen and eggs join together to make seeds. This is called fertilization. When a grain of pollen reaches a flower's stigma, it grows a tube down the style and into the ovary to fertilize the ovule.

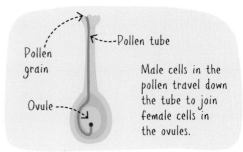

Pollen grain

Pollen tube

Ovule

Male cells in the pollen travel down the tube to join female cells in the ovules.

Fruit

After fertilization, the ovules start to grow into seeds. The flowers die, the petals fall off, and the remaining ovary grows into a fruit while the seeds develop. In some plants, the part below the ovary becomes part of the fruit too.

The development of a cherry fruit

1. As the ovules turn into seeds, the ovary starts to grow and develop fleshy walls.

Ovary

2. By the time the seeds are fully grown, the ripened ovary has developed into a fruit.

Seed

The seed inside the fruit can grow into a new cherry tree.

Looking at seeds

Seeds grow into new plants. For a seed to grow, it needs the right conditions. Fruits disperse (spread) their seeds, so that when the new plants grow, they don't crowd each other, or have to compete for water or light.

Animal dispersal

Many fruits are eaten or carried away by animals. The animals either swallow or drop the seeds. Swallowed seeds pass through an animal's digestive system and are dispersed wherever it poos.

Goosegrass fruits have hooked spikes that stick to animal fur.

This berry's seed will be carried away inside the thrush and planted in its droppings.

This squirrel will bury its acorns but might forget to come back and eat some, leaving them to grow into oak trees.

Wind dispersal

Some plants have lightweight fruits that can be blown away by the wind. Many of these fruits are shaped for flight – some have wings, while others have very fine hairs which act like parachutes to pull the fruit off the plant and carry it away.

Dandelion heads hold many fluffy fruits that act like parachutes.

Poppies have dry seed pods with holes in. The wind blows the pods, shaking out the seeds.

Water dispersal

Some seeds can float away in water. They may travel very long distances before they start to grow.

A water lotus fruit looks like a shower head. It bends down and scatters its seeds into the water.

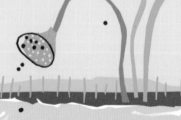

Explosive dispersal

Some plants spread their seeds by exploding. Their fruits are seed pods, which have thin, hard walls. As the walls dry out in the sun and the seeds ripen inside, the pods grow tighter and tighter until they burst open, flinging the seeds far and wide.

Ripe pea pods burst open and hurl out their seeds.

Parts of a seed

Inside a seed is a tiny root and shoot. This is surrounded by a food store that gives it the energy it needs to start growing into a plant.

Kidney beans are a kind of seed. This one has been cut in half to show its insides.

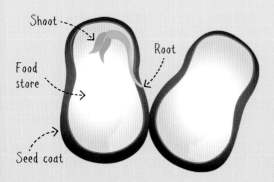

Shoot

Root

Food store

Seed coat

Germination

Germination is when a seed starts growing and a tiny root and shoot begin to sprout. Seeds need water, oxygen and warmth to germinate. They get the energy they need from their food store. It can take weeks for a seed to go through all the stages of germination:

Water

Coat

1. Water enters the seed through a tiny hole in its coat.

2. The seed swells and its coat splits.

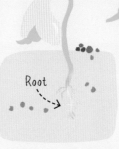

Shoot

Root

3. A root grows down into the soil, anchoring the plant in the ground and seeking water.

4. A little shoot grows up towards the light.

5. The plant's first leaves grow, so it can make its own nutrients.

First leaves

Seeds can survive in the ground for a long time, and will only germinate when there is enough water and light for them to grow.

Find out more about: **leaves** (page 11); **nutrients** (page 6); **roots** (page 10)

Growing plants

Plants need a balance of light, water, carbon dioxide gas and minerals to grow strong and healthy. Too little or too much of these things affects the way plants grow.

Minerals

Minerals are substances found in rocks and soil which all living things need to be healthy. Three minerals are particularly good for plants:

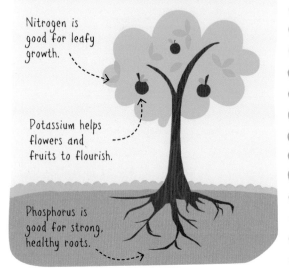

Nitrogen is good for leafy growth.

Potassium helps flowers and fruits to flourish.

Phosphorus is good for strong, healthy roots.

Fertilizers

Healthy soil has most of the nutrients and minerals plants need, but farmers often add extra to the soil in the form of fertilizers, to help their crops grow better. The "plant food" that people sometimes use on house plants is a kind of fertilizer.

Wilting

When plants wilt, they turn yellow and become limp because they have been burned by too much light or haven't had enough water.

Healthy gerbera plant   Wilting gerbera plant

Inside a healthy plant, water fills spaces in its cells, keeping it firm and upright.

Without this water keeping the plant firm, it droops and eventually dies.

Yellowing

Yellowing means turning yellow. This can happen to plants if they don't have enough light, and their leaves can't make enough chlorophyll.

Healthy cress has green leaves that contain chlorophyll.

Yellowing cress

Plants that are yellowing also tend to be tall and spindly. This is because plants grow towards light but, if there's not much available, they grow too quickly, in search of light.

Find out more about: **cells** (page 8); **chlorophyll** (page 11); **nutrients** (page 6); **oxygen** (page 64); **roots** (page 10)

Root rot

A plant's roots can start to rot when it has too much water. Plants take in oxygen from gaps in the soil and if those gaps are filled with water, the roots start to drown and rot. The drowned roots then can't absorb any nutrients from the soil.

Healthy peace lily

Bright green leaves

Healthy roots are yellow and strong.

Peace lily with root rot

Dead leaves

Rotting roots are black and weak.

Symptoms

A sign or effect of a disease is called a symptom.

If a plant has...	it may be a symptom of...
yellow, limp and drooping flowers and leaves	wilting
yellow leaves, and tall, spindly stems	yellowing
green but shrivelled, drooping leaves and blackened roots	root rot

Plant life cycles

A plant's life cycle is the time it takes for it to grow from a seed into an adult, produce seeds of its own, then die. Different types of plants have different lengths of life cycle:

• **Annuals** live and die within a single year. Their whole life may be lived out in just a few weeks.

Marigold   Gypsophila   Morning glory

• **Biennials** take two years to grow and reproduce. They grow and store food in the first year then, in the second year, they produce flowers and seeds.

Foxglove   Evening primrose   Angelica

• **Perennials** can live for many years. Their leaves might fall off from time to time, but other parts, such as their roots or stems, stay alive year after year.

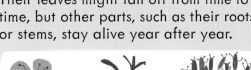

Geranium   Iris   Lavender

• **Ephemerals** grow and reproduce quickly. They often live in very harsh climates where conditions for growth are only right for a very short time.

Desert paintbrush   San Rafael cactus

Looking at animals

All animals are made up of lots of cells. They can't make their own food, like plants do, so get energy by eating plants and other animals. Animals can be divided into groups.

Vertebrates

Vertebrates are a group of animals that have backbones. There are five main types of vertebrate:

Mammals are warm-blooded and hairy. A few types lay eggs, but most females give birth to live babies.

Mammals feed their babies with milk made in their own bodies.

Birds are warm-blooded, feathery animals with two legs and two wings. Females lay eggs with chicks inside. The eggs need to be kept warm until they hatch.

Wing

Feathers

Eggs in nest

18 Find out more about: **cells** (page 8); **organs** (page 9)

Warm-blooded or cold?

Warm-blooded animals can keep their body at one temperature. **Cold-blooded** ones can't – their body temperature depends on how hot or cold their surroundings are.

Reptiles are cold-blooded animals that live on land. They have dry, scaly skin.

Most reptiles lay tough, leathery eggs...

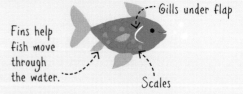

...but some give birth to live young.

Fish are scaly, cold-blooded water animals. They breathe by filtering oxygen from the water through organs called gills.

Gills under flap

Fins help fish move through the water.

Scales

Amphibians are cold-blooded animals that live both in water and on land. Most live in water when they are young, moving onto land as they grow.

Adult toads live on land.

A toad's babies live in water.

Invertebrates

Invertebrates are cold-blooded creatures without backbones. Most have soft, squishy bodies, often with hard shells. There are many different types of invertebrate; here are just some of them:

Arthropods' bodies are made up of sections and are covered by a shell or a hard outer skin. They have six or more jointed legs.

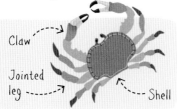

The sections of a crab's body are covered by its shell.

Claw

Jointed leg

Shell

Molluscs need to keep moist to stay alive. They have a soft body with a hard shell either inside or outside their body.

Squid have a shell on the inside of their bodies.

Echinoderms are sea creatures. Their bodies are divided into five identical parts and covered with tough, spiny skin.

You can see the five equal parts of this starfish's body.

Annelids are worms that have bristly bodies made up of ring-shaped segments.

You can see the rings on an earthworm's body, but not its bristles, which are tiny.

Cnidarians have stinging tentacles attached to symmetrical, sack-like bodies. The bodies have just one opening for food and waste.

Jellyfish and coral use their stinging tentacles to paralyse prey.

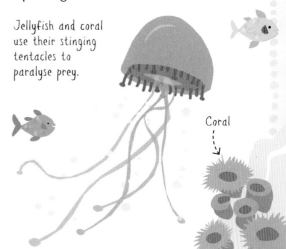

Coral

Sponges are creatures that live on sea beds. They don't have any organs, but are covered in holes that let in water and food.

Sponges attach themselves to sea beds then hardly move at all.

Find out more about: **joints** (page 20); **prey** (page 42)

How animals move

Animals need to move to get food, escape danger and keep healthy. How they move depends on how their body parts, such as muscles, bones and joints, are arranged.

Bones

Bones are hard parts that support an animal's body and help it to move. They also protect its organs and make blood cells. Bones are made up of layers of hard tissue and are strong but also light.

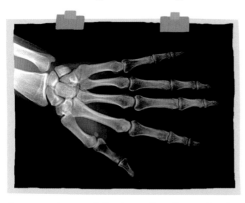

An x-ray image of the bones in a human hand

Skeleton

The different bones in an animal's body are joined together to make a frame called a skeleton.

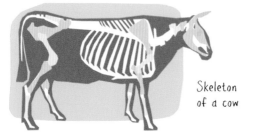

Skeleton of a cow

Joints

A joint is a place where two bones meet. Joints are covered with a rubbery layer and surrounded by fluid to stop the bones from grinding together as they move. Strong bands called **ligaments** join the bones together.

The joints in this swan's neck help it to twist its head around to clean the feathers on its back.

Muscles

Muscles are areas of stretchy tissue inside animals' bodies. They are responsible for all the movements an animal makes, even the ones you can't see from the outside.

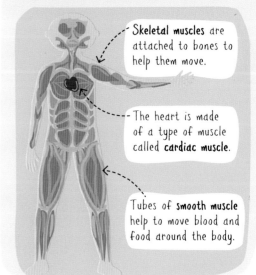

Skeletal muscles are attached to bones to help them move.

The heart is made of a type of muscle called **cardiac muscle**.

Tubes of **smooth muscle** help to move blood and food around the body.

Walking

An animal walks by lifting its feet to take steps. How it walks depends on the number of legs it has:

- Animals with two legs move one leg forwards, then the other leg.

Person walking

- Four-legged animals usually walk by moving diagonally opposite legs at the same time.

Dog walking

1. Move back right and front left leg   2. Move back left and front right leg

- Animals with six legs move one leg on one side of their body and two on the other side all at the same time.

Beetle walking

The legs shown in red are moving.

- Creatures with many legs lift one pair, then the pair behind and so on, all along their bodies.

Millipedes move their legs in a wave-like motion.

Crawling

When an animal crawls, it drags itself along, pushing different parts of its body against the ground to move forwards.

Worms stretch and tighten the muscles in waves along their bodies.

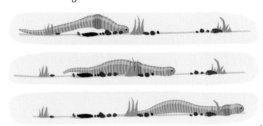

This snake is moving by stretching and tightening different parts of its body at the same time, making S-shaped curves.

Creeping or looping

Some caterpillars creep or loop by arching their bodies, then stretching forwards. While one end of the body moves forwards, the legs at the other end grip onto the surface.

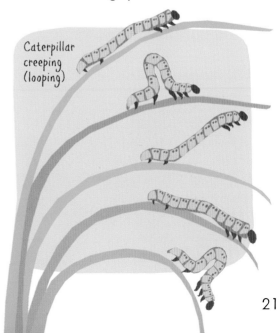

Caterpillar creeping (looping)

Swinging

Some types of monkeys and apes that live in jungles move through the trees by swinging from branch to branch. They use their arms, legs and even tails to grip and pull themselves forwards.

Gibbons swing by stretching out their arms, gripping with their paws, then pulling themselves forwards using their strong shoulder muscles.

Leaping

Leaping means to jump along from a standing position. Animals that leap have back legs that are longer than their front ones. Some animals leap to escape enemies, confusing them by changing direction as they jump.

1. At rest, this frog's legs are bent.

2. It quickly stretches up with great force.

3. It leaps up with straight legs.

Gliding

Gliding is moving through the air by floating on the breeze. Many gliding animals glide for short distances using flaps of skin between their front and back legs. They jump, then stretch their legs to spread out the flaps and catch the air.

Flying lizards don't actually fly, but stretch out flaps of skin to glide from tree to tree.

Flying

Animals that can fly push themselves through the air by moving their wings. The bodies of flying animals have many features that help them stay up in the sky.

Birds have hollow bones, smooth, light feathers, and powerful chest muscles.

Bats have powerful chest muscles and thin, flexible wings.

Insects have light bodies and strong wing muscles.

Swimming

Swimming is travelling through the water by moving parts of the body. Different animals swim in different ways.

Rowing helps many small sea creatures swim. Animals that do this are covered in tiny hairs that they flick back and forth like oars to help them move through the water.

This close-up image of a microscopic sea creature shows the hairs on its body.

Bending their bodies helps many fish swim. They bend in an S-shaped wave that begins at the head and travels down the body towards the tail. This pushes them forwards.

How sharks bend when they swim

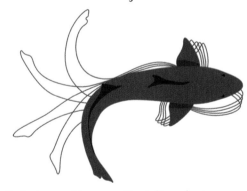

Fish have flaps called **fins** that stick out of their bodies. They use these to push themselves forwards, change direction and stay balanced in the water.

The darker areas show the fish's fins.

Squirting water helps some sea creatures, such as jellyfish, octopuses and squid to swim. They take water into their bodies, then squirt it out quickly in one direction. This pushes them in the opposite direction.

How a jellyfish squirts

1. The jellyfish fills its hollow body with water.

2. It quickly stretches to push out the water and move forward.

Pushing with their flat, stiff wings helps penguins to swim. These broad wings aren't suitable for flying, but are good for pushing through the water and for steering. Penguins steer with their tails and feet, too.

Here are some of the features of a penguin's body that help it to swim well.

Oily feathers to keep water away from its skin

Small, stiff wings to push through the water quickly

Strong muscles in its chest to power its wings

Senses

Animals use sense organs to take in information about the world around them. The information is sent to the brain, which uses it to decide how the animal should react to its surroundings.

Nervous system

The nervous system is a network of thin threads of cells, called nerves. The nerves lead to the brain, carrying messages from the sense organs.

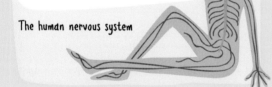

The human nervous system

Touch

An animal's sense of touch lets it know what things feels like. Touch-sensitive cells called receptors near the surface of its body send messages to its brain telling it whether an object is hot or cold, soft or hard, sharp or blunt and so on.

Mammal whiskers and insect antennae are very sensitive to touch.

Whiskers   Antennae

Sight

An animal's sense of sight lets it see what its surroundings look like. An animal sees things because light bounces off objects and enters its eyes. Light-sensitive cells in the eyes pick up information which is turned into pictures by the brain.

An insect's eye is made up of hundreds of tiny parts. Each part detects an image.

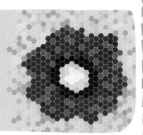

The insect's brain puts all the images together to make a complete picture, like a mosaic.

Many animals' eyes have a hole in the middle called a **pupil**, which widens and narrows to let in different amounts of light. Animals that hunt at night often have large eyes with pupils that can open wide to let in as much light as possible.

Eagles hunt during the day, so their pupils don't need to widen to let in extra light.

Owls hunt at night, so their pupils can open wide to help them see in the dark.

Find out more about: **cells** (page 8); **organs** (page 9);
predators, prey (page 42); **sound waves, vibrations** (page 96)

Smell

Smelling is sensing the scent chemicals that are given off by something. The chemicals go into an animal's body, usually through its nose. Animals use their sense of smell to sniff out food, identify friends and family, and warn them of danger.

Bears have the best sense of smell of any animal – over 2,000 times better than a human's.

A snake detects scents with its tongue, flicking it in and out.

Hearing

Hearing is sensing vibrations called sound waves in the air. This helps animals detect messages from other animals, and pinpoint where things are, such as predators and prey. When sound waves enter an animal's body, they vibrate nerves. The nerves send messages to the brain.

Crickets hear through their legs – a thin surface below their knees vibrates when hit by sound waves.

Rabbits have long ears that can move in different directions to help them pick up even the slightest sound a predator might make.

Taste

Tasting is detecting the flavour of something. Many animals taste with their mouths and tongues; others, such as butterflies, use their feet. Human tongues are covered in tiny bumps called **taste buds**, which send messages to the brain about how something tastes.

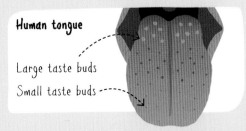

Human tongue

Large taste buds

Small taste buds

As a person chews, their food gives out chemicals that go up into the nose. Together, the nose and taste buds detect the flavour of the food. That's why it's hard to taste anything when you have a blocked nose.

Tasting something helps an animal know whether or not it's safe to eat. Rotten food and most poisonous things taste horrible, so animals avoid eating them.

Any predator that tries to put this poison dart frog in its mouth would spit it out because it tastes so revolting.

Teeth

Teeth break food down into pieces, making it easy to swallow. Many vertebrate animals have teeth.

Parts of a tooth

Most types of teeth have three main parts: a crown, a neck and a root.

Crown – this is the part above the gum. It's covered with a very hard and often shiny layer of **enamel**, which protects the inside of the tooth. Soft **pulp** inside the crown contains nerve endings and the tooth's blood supply. The rest of the tooth is a tough substance called **dentine**.

Neck – this is where the crown meets the parts below the gums.

Root – this holds the tooth in place in the jaw bones. Roots contain nerves and blood vessels. A tooth can have one, two or three roots.

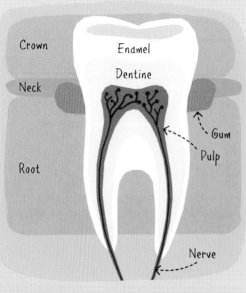

Crown

Enamel

Dentine

Neck

Gum

Pulp

Root

Nerve

Types of teeth

The type of teeth an animal has depends on the food it eats.

Lions are hunters and meat-eaters, so have sharp teeth for killing and eating their food.

Sheep just eat plants, so have flat teeth for grinding.

People can eat both meat and plants, so they have some teeth that are sharp and others that are flat.

Each type of tooth has a different name:

Molars are broad, square teeth with points and grooves that help animals to chew and grind food.

Premolars are thin, square teeth with two points. Animals use them to mash and grind food.

Canines are long, cone-shaped teeth with a sharp point that helps animals to pierce and tear meat.

Incisors are flat-topped, small, front teeth that help animals to cut food or scrape meat from bones.

Find out more about: **blood vessels** (page 33); **nerves** (page 24); **vertebrates** (page 18)

Sets of teeth

A set of teeth is all the teeth an animal is using in its mouth. Many animals grow new teeth to replace ones that fall out and some replace whole sets.

Most mammals, like humans, have two sets of teeth during their lives. Young mammals have **baby teeth** but, as the animals grow, their baby teeth gradually fall out and are replaced by bigger, stronger **adult teeth**.

A newborn horse's front baby teeth

A 15-year-old horse's front adult teeth

Most sharks have lots of rows of teeth. A shark's tooth doesn't have roots, so breaks off easily, usually lasting for about a week before it falls out. Then, the tooth behind it moves up to replace it. Sharks keep replacing their teeth all their lives.

Broken tooth

Plaque

Plaque is a sticky covering that forms over teeth. It is made when bacteria in an animal's mouth feed off sugary foods stuck to teeth. This makes an acid which dissolves teeth and damages gums, causing **tooth decay** and **gum disease**.

Tooth decay

1. Acid makes a hole in the tooth's enamel.

2. If the hole reaches the nerves, the tooth hurts.

3. Decay and infection can rot the whole tooth.

Gum disease

1. Plaque builds up between the teeth.

2. The gum becomes infected. It bleeds.

3. The gum shrinks, and the teeth fall out.

Dental hygiene

Dental hygiene means keeping teeth healthy. Wild animals scrape plaque off their teeth when they tear at their food. But people need to brush their teeth using a toothpaste that strengthens enamel and repairs damage caused by plaque.

Find out more about: **bacteria** (page 40); **mammals** (page 18)

Eating

The food that animals eat contains the nutrients they need to give them energy. The energy is released inside an animal's body.

Animal diets

What an animal eats is called its diet. Some animals stay healthy by eating just one type of food; others need a mixture of different types.

Omnivores need a mixture of nutrients, so can eat both plants and meat.

Carnivores eat only or mainly meat. They wouldn't get the energy they need if they ate just plants.

Herbivores can only eat plants, and would become ill if they ate meat.

Digestion

As food passes through an animal's body, it goes through a series of organs, being broken down into pieces to release its energy. This is called digestion.

Organs fish use for digestion

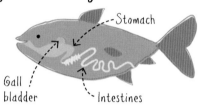

Stomach

Gall bladder

Intestines

Animals that eat different types of food usually use more organs for digestion than those that eat just one type.

Organs humans use for digestion

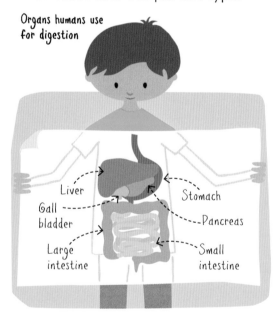

Liver

Gall bladder

Large intestine

Stomach

Pancreas

Small intestine

Mouth

In mammals, food starts being broken down in the mouth. A mammal chews its food using its teeth and softens it with a clear liquid called **saliva** that is made inside the mouth.

Stomach

In many animals, after the food has been eaten, it enters the stomach. Here, digestive juices and powerful muscles start breaking it down and churning it into a thick liquid. Acids in the stomach kill bacteria in the food.

Starfish have two stomachs – they can push one of them out of their mouth to start digesting food even before they've swallowed it.

Stomach

Mouth

Intestines

When food leaves the stomach it goes to the intestines. Some animals' intestines are very simple.

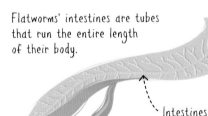

Flatworms' intestines are tubes that run the entire length of their body.

Intestines

Other animals, such as mammals and fish, have intestines that contain juices that are made in organs called the liver, pancreas and gall bladder. The juices break up the different parts of the food, which then pass into the body's blood supply.

Waste

Any water or parts of food that can't been absorbed by the intestines are called waste. It is pushed out of the body as wee and poo.

Bird pellets

Bird pellets are bundles of undigested food coughed up by meat-eating birds, such as owls and eagles. These birds swallow their prey whole.

It can be a struggle for meat-eating birds to fit bigger prey into their mouths.

The parts that are too tough to be digested, such as fur and bones, squash into pellets in a bird's stomach and are coughed up out of its mouth.

You can see bones, fur and feathers in this pellet.

Energy

Animals need energy from food so they can move around and keep the insides of their bodies running smoothly, doing jobs such as making new cells and fighting diseases.

Find out more about: **bacteria** (page 40); **mammals** (page 18); **nutrients** (page 6); **organs** (page 9)

Food groups

A food group is a collection of foods with particular nutrients in them that animals need to grow and thrive. People need to eat foods from all the groups to stay healthy.

Carbohydrates

Carbohydrates are foods that give energy. During digestion they are broken down inside the body into **glucose**, which the body uses as fuel to make energy. There are two main types of carbohydrates:

Sugars are sweet and dissolve in water. The body absorbs them easily, and quickly turns them into glucose.

Starches don't dissolve in water. It takes longer for the body to absorb them so energy is released more gradually.

The glucose that your body doesn't need is stored as body fat, so eating too many carbohydrates can cause weight problems.

Fibre

Fibre is a substance found in plant cells. Eating fibre helps an animal pass waste out of its body. Fibre makes the waste soft and bulky, which helps it to travel out of the body without getting stuck.

Fruit, vegetables, cereals, nuts and brown bread all contain a lot of fibre.

Proteins

Proteins are substances that help build and repair an animal's body tissue and keep it in good condition. An animal needs protein to help build up its muscles and organs, and to help it fight disease.

Meat and fish, as well as dairy products, nuts and beans, each contain a different type of protein.

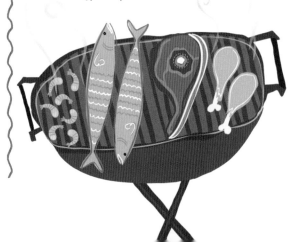

Find out more about: **cells** (page 8); **digestion** (page 28); **organs** (page 9); **tissue** (page 9)

Fats

Animals need a certain amount of fat in their bodies to store energy, keep the body warm, protect the organs and build cells. There are two types of fats: **unsaturated fats** and **saturated fats.**

Unsaturated fats are in plant products, such as...

...olive oil   ...nuts   ...avocados

Saturated fats are in animal products, such as...

...red meat   ...butter   ...milk

Unsaturated fat is good for you in small amounts. Large amounts of some types of saturated fat can cause weight gain, and may increase the risk of heart disease.

Water

All types of food contain water. Animals need water to:

- transport food and oxygen to all their body cells;
- remove waste from their bodies;
- protect their joints and organs;
- help them stay at the same temperature, if they're warm-blooded.

Vitamins

A vitamin is a mixture of different natural chemicals that an animal needs in a very small amount. Here are some of the ways different vitamins help the parts of the body:

Vitamin	Found in	Good for
A	Milk, butter, eggs, green vegetables	Eyesight, skin
B	Brown bread and rice, yeast, soya beans	Energy levels, blood cells
C	Oranges, tomatoes, lemons, blackcurrants	Resisting infection
D	Milk, eggs, butter, oily fish	Bones, teeth
E	Nuts and seeds, eggs, brown bread and rice	Eyes, skin, liver, lungs

Minerals

A mineral is a natural chemical that plants absorb through the soil and that animals get by eating plants. Here are some of the ways minerals help the parts of the body:

Mineral	Found in	Good for
Calcium	Dairy products, green vegetables	Bones, teeth
Iron	Red meat, fish, eggs, beans, dried fruit	Transporting oxygen in blood
Potassium	Bananas, tomatoes, green vegetables, beans, peas, dried fruit	Muscles, nervous system

Find out more about: **nervous system** (page 24); **warm-blooded** (page 18); **waste** (page 29)

Circulation

To stay alive, animals need to move oxygen, food and waste around their bodies. This is called circulation. Substances are often carried around an animal's body in its blood.

Circulatory system

An animal's circulatory system is made up of all the parts involved in circulation, including blood, blood-carrying tubes, and at least one heart. In some animals, such as mammals, lungs are part of the circulatory system too.

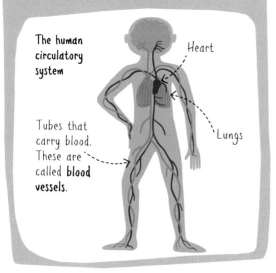

The human circulatory system

Heart

Lungs

Tubes that carry blood. These are called **blood vessels**.

Single and double

Fish have **single circulation**. Their blood flows through their heart once in its journey around the body. Most other animals have **double circulation**. Their blood flows through their heart twice.

Blood

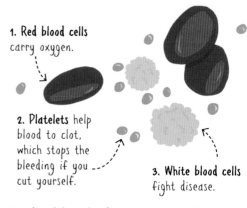

Blood is a mixture of different cells floating in liquid in an animal's body. It has many important jobs including:

- carrying food, oxygen and cell waste (chemicals that cells don't want any more) around the body
- controlling body temperature
- fighting germs
- healing wounds

Close-up of cells in human blood

Many animals' blood is red because it's mostly made up of red coloured cells. These cells are purplish, but turn red when they absorb oxygen.

1. Red blood cells carry oxygen.

2. Platelets help blood to clot, which stops the bleeding if you cut yourself.

3. White blood cells fight disease.

In the blood of most invertebrates, the cells that transport oxygen don't turn red. An invertebrate's blood can be colourless, yellow, blue or green.

Amphibians have greenish blood because it contains a green liquid called bile.

Heart

An animal's heart is a powerful, muscly organ that pumps blood. Every time a heart beats, it squeezes out blood, sending it racing to all the different parts of the body.

How blood flows through a human heart

| Blood returning from body without oxygen | Blood going to lungs without oxygen | Blood going to body with oxygen | Blood returning from lungs with oxygen |

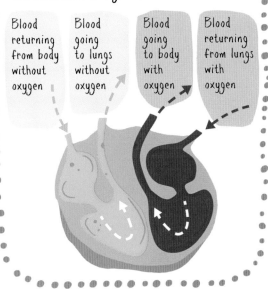

Blood vessels

• **Arteries** are blood vessels that lead away from the heart.

• **Veins** carry blood back to the heart from the rest of the body.

• **Capillaries** are the smallest blood vessels, which connect arteries and veins to the body's cells. They have thin walls, so that food, oxygen and waste can pass through them.

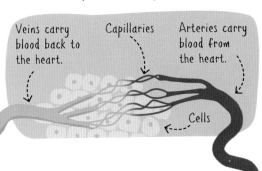

Veins carry blood back to the heart.

Capillaries

Arteries carry blood from the heart.

Cells

Lungs

Lungs are spongy organs that take in air when an animal breathes. Animal cells need oxygen from the air to release energy from food.

How a person's lungs help to circulate oxygen

1. Air goes into the lungs when the person takes a breath in.

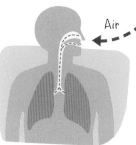

Air

2. Inside the lungs, oxygen is separated out from the rest of the gases in the air.

3. The oxygen passes through the lung walls into the red blood cells in capillaries running close by.

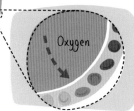

Oxygen

Pulse

You can feel the blood pumping through your body where your blood vessels are closest to your skin. These are your pulse points.

You can press gently on your pulse points to feel your blood pumping – there are two points in your arm.

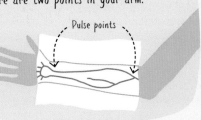

Pulse points

Find out more about: **organs** (page 9); **oxygen** (page 64)

Keeping healthy

Keeping your body healthy is a matter of staying active, eating the right foods, fighting illness and staying away from substances that are harmful.

Balanced diet

Having a balanced diet means eating a variety of foods in the right amounts from all the food groups. People with balanced diets take in all the nutrients they need to stay healthy, and don't eat too many of the things that might make them unhealthy, such as fats and sugars.

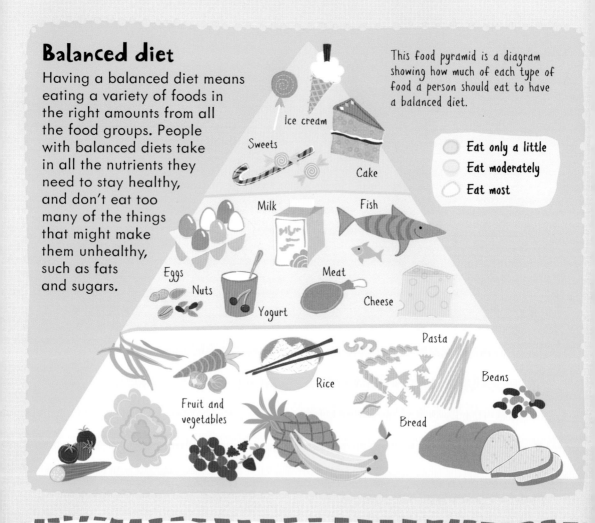

This food pyramid is a diagram showing how much of each type of food a person should eat to have a balanced diet.

Ice cream

Sweets

Cake

Eat only a little

Eat moderately

Eat most

Milk

Fish

Eggs

Nuts

Meat

Cheese

Yogurt

Rice

Pasta

Beans

Fruit and vegetables

Bread

Drugs

A drug is anything a person takes to affect the way the body works. Too much of any drug can be harmful.

• Some drugs are medicines. A doctor tells you how much to take to help you feel better when you're ill.

• Some drugs, such as heroin and cocaine, are so dangerous that they're completely illegal.

• Others, such as alcohol and nicotine, are only legal to take if you're over a certain age, but they're still harmful.

34 Find out more about: **food groups** (pages 30-31); **nutrients** (page 6)

Addiction

If you're addicted to something, you feel that you need it, even if it's harmful. Going without it would make you upset or even physically ill. Many drugs are addictive.

Alcohol

Alcohol is a liquid drug that is mixed with other ingredients to make alcoholic drinks.

Good effect	Bad effect
• Can make you feel relaxed and happy	• Can make you feel sad or angry
• Can make you feel part of a group	• Can make you do silly or dangerous things
	• Can badly damage your liver, brain and heart
	• Can be addictive

Nicotine

Nicotine is a chemical drug in the tobacco plant. People smoke tobacco through cigarettes or cigars. This sends the nicotine into their lungs.

Good effect	Bad effect
• Can make you feel relaxed	• Can cause headaches and dizziness
• Can make you feel energetic	• Smoking tobacco can badly damage your mouth, throat, lungs and heart
	• Can be addictive

Exercise

Exercising means moving around and doing a particular set of actions to:

- keep your body flexible
- build up your muscles
- strengthen your heart and lungs
- control or lose weight

Using your muscles makes you build new muscle tissue to help with the work you're making your body do.

Working your joints strengthens them and helps them to move more freely.

When exercising, you breathe more deeply to take in more oxygen. This strengthens your lungs.

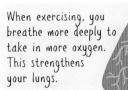

Your heart gets stronger during exercise as it beats faster to pump your blood.

Exercise sends oxygen to the fat stores in your body. It breaks down the fat to release energy.

Find out more about: **heart** (page 33); **lungs** (page 33); **oxygen** (page 64)

Reproduction

All organisms can reproduce to create more of their own kind. Most animals pair up to do this, in a couple made of one male and one female.

Mating

Mating is when a male and female animal join together to reproduce. Female sex cells have to join with the male ones for new life to form.

Butterflies mate by joining the ends of their bodies together.

Eggs

Eggs contain female sex cells and are made by female animals. Some babies develop from eggs inside their mothers' bodies. Others grow inside eggs that the mother has pushed out of her body.

Women make eggs in their **ovaries** – the eggs are released into an organ called the **uterus**.

(not to scale)

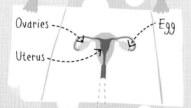

Ovaries

Egg

Uterus

Sperm

Sperm is the male sex cell. Males release lots of sperm at once, but it only takes one sperm to join with one egg for a new life to be created.

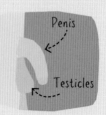

Penis

Testicles

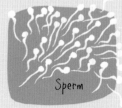

Sperm

A man's reproductive organs hang outside his body.

Sperm is made in the testicles and travels to the penis.

Fertilization

Fertilization is when a male sex cell joins with a female sex cell and creates the beginnings of a new organism. This happens inside the female's body, or after the female has laid the eggs.

A man's sperm reaches a woman's egg by travelling through his penis and into the woman's uterus.

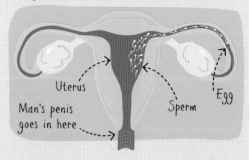

Uterus

Man's penis goes in here

Sperm

Egg

Female fish release their eggs into the water, then males squirt sperm on top to fertilize them.

Eggs

36

Find out more about: **cells** (page 8); **organs** (page 9)

Embryo

Fertilization creates an embryo – a new life in early development. Embryos develop quickly, growing from a few cells to organisms with basic organs and systems.

Birds and reptiles go through their embryo stage while they're developing inside their eggs.

Humans are described as embryos for about the first eight weeks after fertilization.

(not to scale)

Foetus

A foetus is an unborn baby inside its mother's body at the later stages of development. An embryo starts being described as a foetus when it has begun to develop all its organs and body parts.

By the time an elephant foetus has been inside its mother for six months, it has developed all its main body parts.

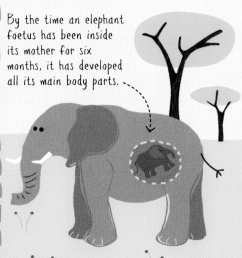

Hatching

A baby animal that has grown inside an egg has to hatch out when it has developed enough to survive outside. It chips away at the shell from the inside, gradually breaking the egg open and pushing itself out.

Egg tooth

1. A baby turtle is inside this egg, and ready to hatch out.

2. It uses an "egg tooth" on its nose to chip at its shell.

3. It pushes at the hole in the shell to make it bigger.

4. It breaks out of the shell and scuttles away.

Birth

When a baby animal that has been growing inside its mother's body has developed enough to survive outside, it is pushed out. This is called birth.

The mother pushes the baby out using muscles inside her body. The muscles tighten and relax in movements called **contractions**. The time it takes for the baby to be pushed out is called **labour**.

Most insects lay eggs, but aphids give birth to live young instead.

Find out more about: **systems** (page 9)

Life cycles

Animals go through lots of changes during their life. Patterns in the way they grow and behave in the time between birth and death are called a life cycle.

Life span

An animal's life span is the time it normally takes for it to complete its life cycle. Some animals take years to complete their life cycle; others last for just a few weeks.

Human life cycle

Humans grow, but their body shape stays roughly the same as they go through their life cycle.

Infant – a baby in the earliest stage of development after being born and before it can walk or talk

Child – a young, growing person whose body isn't ready for reproduction yet

Adolescent – a young person who is nearly fully developed and whose body is changing so that he or she can reproduce

Adult – a fully grown person who can reproduce to create an infant

Insect life cycles

Some insects not only change size but also change shape as they go from one life cycle stage to the next.

Butterfly life cycle

1. Embryo – a developing baby insect growing inside an egg

2. Larva – a young, growing insect that has hatched out of its egg (plural: larvae)

Lays eggs

4. Adult – a fully grown insect

3. Pupa – a young insect that is changing into its adult shape inside a protective coating

Instead of going through the larva and pupa stages, some insects become **nymphs** – young insects that hatch out of their eggs looking like smaller versions of their parents.

Grasshopper life cycle

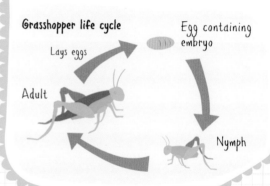

Lays eggs

Egg containing embryo

Adult

Nymph

Find out more about: **eggs** (page 36); **reproduction** (pages 36-37)

Amphibian life cycle

Young amphibians live in water but then move onto land as adults. They return to the water to lay eggs.

Frog life cycle

1. Embryo - a developing baby amphibian that is growing inside an egg

2. Larva (called tadpole) - a young, growing amphibian that has hatched out of its egg

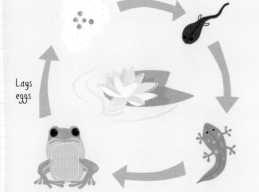

Lays eggs

4. Adult - a fully grown amphibian

3. Juvenile - a young amphibian that has started to develop adult body parts and features

Hibernation

Hibernation is part of some animals' **annual cycle**. These are the changes that happen to it over one year.

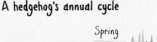

A hedgehog's annual cycle

Spring

Hibernating in undergrowth

Eating to build up strength

Winter

Summer

Autumn

Hibernating in undergrowth

Mating and having babies

Hibernation is when an animal goes into a deep sleep during winter because there isn't much food for it to eat. Its temperature drops, and its heartbeat and breathing slow down so that it doesn't use much energy.

Migration

At some stage in their life cycles, many animals gather with others of their kind to make a long journey to find a place to feed or mate.

This is called migration. Some animals only migrate once in their lifetime; others travel these long distances as often as twice a year.

Salmon life cycle

Young salmon migrate to sea.

Salmon grow into adults in sea.

Babies grow in river.

Adults lay and fertilize eggs in river.

Adults return to river.

Find out more about: **amphibians** (page 18); **mating** (page 36)

Micro-organisms

Some living things are so small that you can only see them using a microscope. They're usually made up of one cell and are called microbes or micro-organisms.

Viruses

Viruses are the smallest of all organisms and are only alive when they're inside another living thing. They can harm the thing they're living inside, and cause common illnesses, such as colds and chickenpox, as well as more serious ones such as yellow fever and rabies.

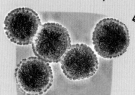

This is what the influenza (flu) virus looks like under a very powerful microscope.

Bacteria

Bacteria are simple cells that live in the air, the ground and living things. Some types are useful, for example there are bacteria inside people's bodies that help them digest food. Others can cause illnesses.

These round bacteria cause food poisoning.

These sausage-shaped bacteria cause pneumonia.

These spiral bacteria cause rat-bite fever.

Protozoa

Protozoa are single cells that are similar to animal cells. Some cause diseases, such as dysentery and malaria. They eat smaller organisms, such as bacteria, by wrapping themselves around their prey then swallowing them up.

How protozoa feed...

1. To reach its prey, this protozoan pushes part of itself forward.

2. It oozes around its prey and surrounds it.

3. The prey is swallowed up, broken down and absorbed.

Algae

Algae are simple organisms that make their own food by photosynthesis. They are most commonly found in water but can grow in any damp places.

This microscopic diatom is one of the simplest types of algae. It lives as a single, individual cell.

Other algae can join together in strands to form seaweeds.

40 Find out more about: **cells** (page 8); **oxygen** (page 64); **photosynthesis** (page 11)

Fungi

Fungi are simple organisms that are closely related to plants. They often grow in dark, damp places and feed off other living organisms or rotting things.

Mould

Moulds are simple, tiny fungi that grow in masses called colonies.

Mould often looks fuzzy or slimy and grows on rotting food and on damp walls and ceilings. It can be any colour.

Fruit contains lots of moisture, so becomes mouldy quickly.

Toasted bread is dry, so takes longer than fruit to become mouldy.

Mildew

Mildew is usually grey or white and looks powdery or feathery. You can find it growing on damp or old paper and fabrics. It also infects plants, coating their leaves with a light-coloured powder.

A white, powdery mildew is growing on this rose plant.

Toadstools and mushrooms

Toadstools and mushrooms are general names for fungi that grow a fleshy cap on a stalk. Like many fungi, they make tiny cells called spores. These blow away in the breeze and grow into new fungi.

Fly agaric toadstool

Cap

Spores are made here.

Spores

Stalk

Mesh of root-like threads

There's no scientific difference between a mushroom and a toadstool, but fungi that are safe to eat often have "mushroom" in their name. Be careful, though, as some fungi that are called mushrooms are actually poisonous.

This death cap mushroom is very poisonous.

Habitats

The type of environment where an organism lives in the wild is called its habitat. Living things become well suited to their habitat and come to depend on the other organisms that live there.

Ecosystems

Many different organisms live in one habitat, from tiny bacteria to big, powerful hunters. The living things in a habitat plus the habitat itself are called an ecosystem.

Adaptation

Over time, living things slowly change to become more suited to the conditions of their habitat. This is called adaptation.

Polar bears have developed thick fur and a layer of fat to keep out the cold of their Arctic habitat.

The thick trunk of a saguro cactus can expand to store as much water as possible on the rare occasions when it rains in its desert habitat.

Producers and consumers

Organisms in a habitat are either producers or consumers. Those such as plants and algae that make their own food by photosynthesis are **producers**. Those that eat producers, and the things that eat those organisms are **consumers**.

Seaweed makes its own food by photosynthesis so it is a producer.

Green sea turtles eat seaweed so they are consumers.

Tiger sharks eat sea turtles so they are consumers, too.

Predators and prey

Animals in a habitat can be predators or prey (or both). A **predator** is an animal that hunts and kills other animals for food. The animals that it eats are its **prey**.

A lion is a predator on the African grasslands...

...and a warthog is one of its prey.

Scavengers

Scavengers are carnivores that eat animals that have died naturally or been killed by a predator. They don't usually kill prey themselves.

Vultures have sharp vision so they can spot a dead animal from high up.

Hyenas have strong teeth and jaws to crunch through the bones of dead animals.

Interdependence

Many organisms in a habitat rely on each other and their environment to stay alive. This is called interdependence.

Decomposers

Decomposers feed on dead or rotting plants and animals, breaking them down into simple nutrients and causing them to decay. The nutrients are released into the soil, air and water, where plants can use them to grow. Worms, fungi and bacteria are decomposers.

Earthworms and fungi break down dead or rotting plants as they absorb nutrients from them.

Food chain

A food chain is a diagram showing how energy passes between organisms within a habitat when one eats another. The chain starts with a producer and ends with a top consumer – one that nothing else eats.

This food chain from an Australian forest habitat shows that grass is eaten by mice, and mice are eaten by eagles.

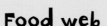

Food web

A food web is a number of food chains that are linked to each other, showing the interdependence of lots of different types of organisms in a habitat.

This food web shows the connections between different living things in an Australian forest habitat.

Wedge-tailed eagle

Snake

Kookaburra

Mouse

Rabbit

Grasshopper

Grass

Find out more about: **bacteria** (page 40); **carnivores** (page 28); **fungi** (page 41); **organisms** (page 7); **photosynthesis** (page 11)

Biomes

Biomes are big ecosystems (see page 42). Each kind of biome has particular weather patterns and contains plants and animals that are suited to the environment.

Coniferous forest

Coniferous forests are cool all year round and most of the trees there have needle-shaped leaves. These forests are found in North America, Europe and Asia.

Most coniferous trees stay green all year long. They often have cones to hold their seeds.

Tropical rainforest

Tropical forests are hot and wet throughout the year. They grow in South America, southern Asia, Africa and Australia.

Tropical forests are home to many brightly coloured animals.

Deciduous forest

Deciduous forests are warm in summer and cold in winter. They grow in central Europe, North America, Asia and Australia. Many of the animals that live there migrate to warmer places in winter.

In summer, deciduous trees are green.

By winter, all their leaves have fallen off.

Mountains

Mountains are high, peaked areas that are bare and cold at the top. There are more plants and animals further down a mountain, where it's warmer. The very highest mountains are in Asia and South America.

Mountain goats are good climbers and have a thick coat to keep them warm.

Find out more about: **migration** (page 39)

Grasslands

Grasslands are huge open areas with grasses, low plants and bushes, and only a few trees. There are two types of grasslands:

Tropical grasslands are in places that are hot and have rainy seasons, such as South America, Africa and Asia.

Tropical grasslands have enough rain for trees to grow.

Temperate grasslands are dry with hot summers and cold winters. They grow in North America, Europe and Asia.

The dry weather of temperate grasslands means only small plants and a few trees can grow.

Tundra

Tundra is bare, sometimes rocky, ground at the very northernmost parts of America and Europe. The ground is frozen all year round.

Musk oxen stay warm in the frozen tundra because they have the longest, thickest fur of any animal.

Deserts

Deserts are areas of land that are so dry that very little can survive there. The biggest deserts are in Africa, the east of Asia, and Australia.

Scorpions are covered by a tough outer layer to protect their insides from the scorching desert heat.

Oceans

Oceans cover most of the Earth's surface. They can be warm or cold, depending on where they are in the world. The further down into an ocean you go, the darker it becomes. Each layer of the ocean is home to different types of creatures.

Turtles splash around in the brightest, top ocean layer.

Octopuses swim in the dimly-lit, middle ocean layer.

Glowing angler fish lurk in the darkest ocean depths.

Materials

Everything in the universe, from a grain of sand to the biggest star, is made of stuff. In science, types of stuff are called materials.

Substance

Substance is another name for material. Objects, powders and liquids are all substances.

Physical characteristics

The physical characteristics, or **physical properties**, of a material are the ways it behaves and the things about it that make it useful. They help you describe exactly what it is and decide what to use it for.

A car is made of different materials, each with its own physical characteristics.

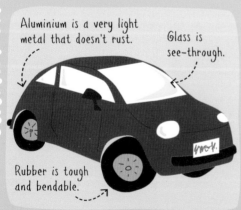

Aluminium is a very light metal that doesn't rust.

Glass is see-through.

Rubber is tough and bendable.

There are two types of physical characteristics – qualitative and quantitative.

Qualitative characteristics

Qualitative characteristics are often very obvious things that you can easily find out about a material by using your senses.

Some qualitative characteristics	
Appearance	What does it look like? What colour is it? Is it shiny or dull?
Taste	Does it have a taste? What kind? (For example, is it sweet, salty, bitter...? Does the taste remind you of something else?)
Smell	Does it have a smell? What kind? (For example, is it fresh, flowery, sweet, rotten...? Does it remind you of something else?)
Feel	What does it feel like? Is it rough or smooth? Is it soft or hard?
Sound	If you tap it with your nails, how does it sound? (For example, does it make a bright "ting", or a dull tap or thump?)

Another interesting physical characteristic is whether light can travel through a material. If it can, the material is described as transparent. If light can't shine through, the material is opaque.

Glass is transparent – you can see through it.

A backpack is opaque – you can't see inside.

Quantitative characteristics

A quantitative characteristic is something about a material that can be measured and a value given to it.

Mass – Placing a material on a set of scales will tell you its mass – that is, how heavy or light it is. The heavier a material is, the more it weighs.

Weighing cake ingredients such as flour and butter will tell you their mass.

Freezing, melting and boiling points – Most materials freeze, melt and boil at certain temperatures, called their freezing, melting and boiling points. They are measured with a thermometer.

The temperature at which a material freezes is called its freezing point. Water freezes into ice at 0°C.

The temperature at which a material melts is called its melting point. Ice melts at 0°C, turning to water.

A material boils at a temperature called its boiling point. Water boils at 100°C, turning to steam.

Other quantitative characteristics

These characteristics can all be measured and given a value.

Malleable	It can be bent into different shapes. Clay is malleable.
Ductile	It can be stretched out into a wire. Many metals are ductile.
Flexible	It can be folded or twisted. Rubber is flexible.
Rigid	It can't be bent, squashed or squeezed. Concrete is rigid.
Fragile	It is easy to break or shatter. Glass is fragile.
Strong	It does not break easily. Iron is strong.
Soluble	It can dissolve in a liquid. Sugar is soluble in water.
Insoluble	It can't dissolve in a liquid. Sand is insoluble in water.
Buoyant	It can float. Cork is buoyant.
Non-buoyant	It sinks. Lead is non-buoyant.
Absorbent	It soaks up liquid easily. Cotton wool is absorbent.
Non-absorbent /waterproof	It doesn't soak up liquid at all. Rubber is waterproof.

Using materials

Materials have different properties and so they can be used for different jobs. Investigating their characteristics can help you decide what material to use for which purpose.

Plastic is strong, buoyant and waterproof – so it's perfect for making into baby bath toys.

Find out more about: **freezing** (page 60); **insoluble** (page 66); **mass** (page 72); **melting** (page 60); **soluble** (page 66); **temperature** (page 50); **thermometers** (page 94)

Hardness and flexibility

Some materials are soft and squashy, others are tough and hard. They can also be strong or fragile, and flexible or rigid. The combination of properties makes materials useful for different things.

Hardness

A material is hard if it can't easily be scratched, dented or squeezed into another shape. Hard materials are tough and firm to touch.

Diamond is the hardest material on Earth. You can only scratch a diamond using another diamond.

This powerful drill has a steel point that is extremely strong and sharp so it can crack the hard stone.

Fragile

A fragile material breaks or tears easily and can't support heavy loads. If a material isn't strong it is described as weak or fragile.

Softness

Soft materials can be gentle to the touch, such as those used in cuddly toys. It is often easy to squeeze or squidge them and alter their shape.

A ball of wool is soft because it can be squashed and squeezed, and the wool itself feels gentle to the touch.

In science, even some things that seem solid and hard can also be described as soft. These are materials that can be scratched and bent.

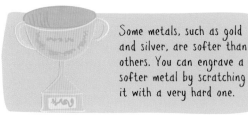

Some metals, such as gold and silver, are softer than others. You can engrave a softer metal by scratching it with a very hard one.

Strength

The strength of a material is how heavy a load it can carry, or how hard you can pull on it, without it breaking or tearing. The more weight a material can deal with, the stronger it is.

A paper bag is strong enough that it can easily carry light clothes.

The same bag will soon tear if you put too many heavy tin cans in it.

Flexible

The shape of flexible materials can easily be changed. If you can bend, fold, twist and turn a material, it is flexible. Fabrics are very flexible materials.

Elastic hairbands are very flexible, so you can stretch and twist them.

A ruler is slightly flexible but if you bend it too much it will break.

There are several ways that a material can be flexible. Here are some words that describe different kinds of flexibility.

Describing flexibility

Squashy	A squashy material, such as sponge, can be pressed to make it smaller.
Bendy	Bendy materials, such as paper, can be easily folded or curved. A material that can't be bent is stiff.
Twistable	A twistable material can be wound around itself. Rope is twistable. Some materials, such as a tissue, are stronger when they are twisted.
Stretchy	A stretchy material can be pulled out to be longer than its original shape. Chewing gum is stretchy.
Springy	Springy materials quickly change back to their original shape if they've been stretched out. Rubber bands are springy.

Rigid

The shape of rigid materials can't easily be changed. A material that can't be squashed, squeezed, bent, stretched or twisted, is a rigid material.

The frame of a bike needs to be rigid to carry a person without changing shape. It's made of rigid metal.

A plant pot is rigid. You want it to keep its shape and not be squashed or stretched as the plants grow.

Suitable materials

A suitable material is one that is perfect for a particular job. What materials are used for will depend on their properties, such as strength, hardness and flexibility.

A brick is hard and strong.

A glass bottle is hard but fragile.

A paper tissue is soft and fragile.

A canvas bag is soft but strong.

Find out more about: **fabrics** (page 53); **springs** (page 80)

Materials and heat

The way that materials behave at different temperatures, and how well they carry heat, helps people decide what to use them for.

Temperature

Temperature is a measure of how hot or cold something is. You use a thermometer to measure temperature in units called degrees Celsius (°C) or degrees Fahrenheit (°F).

Thermometer ------>

1,000°C (1,832°F) is the temperature of a candle flame.

At 100°C (212°F) water boils, and turns to steam.

40°C (104°F) is about the temperature of a hot bath.

The temperature of the air on a hot day is about 32°C (90°F).

3°C (37°F) is the temperature you'd expect inside a fridge.

At 0°C (32°F) water turns to ice, and ice turns to water.

On snowy days the temperature is often below -2°C (28°F).

The temperature inside a freezer is about -17°C (1°F).

Arctic winter temperatures fall to about -40°C (-40°F).

°C
110
100
90
80
70
60
50
40
30
20
10
0
-10
-20

Hot and cold

When a material is hot, it has a lot of heat. A cold material doesn't have much heat. Another name for heat is thermal energy.

This steaming bathwater has lots of thermal energy so it is very warm.

These chilly ice cubes, straight from the freezer, haven't much thermal energy at all.

Expansion

When something expands, it gets bigger. Some materials become a little bigger when they are heated up. This is called expansion.

Some thermometers have liquids inside them that expand as they get hotter, and shrink as they get colder.

As the liquid inside a thermometer gets warmer, it expands, and moves up the tube. The scale shows the temperature.

Road bridges are built with expansion joints in them. These have spaces in them that allow the road material to expand on hot days without bending the road surface.

 Find out more about: **heat** (pages 94-95); **melting** (page 60); **thermometers** (page 94)

Contraction

When something contracts, it gets smaller. Some materials become a little smaller when they are cooled. This is called contraction. It is the opposite of expansion.

On a warm day, power cables expand, and hang loosely between pylons.

On a cold day, they contract and are stretched more tightly.

Moving heat

Heat always travels from a hotter material to a cooler material, and never the other way around. You can find out more about how heat moves on page 95.

Heat from the hot drink is moving into the cold spoon and warming it up.

Thermal conductors

Some materials let heat move through them easily. They are called thermal conductors. Metals are good thermal conductors.

This metal saucepan conducts heat well so the food inside it quickly gets hotter.

Thermal insulators

Some materials do not conduct heat well. These materials are called thermal insulators. Plastics, wood and some fabrics are good thermal insulators. They keep heat in.

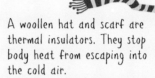

A woollen hat and scarf are thermal insulators. They stop body heat from escaping into the cold air.

Feathers, body fat and fur are great thermal insulators that help to keep animals warm in freezing conditions.

A thermos flask is a thermal insulator because the shiny surface reflects the heat of the liquid and keeps it inside.

Heat is trapped in here.

Air acts as a thermal insulator.

Hot drinks are often served in polystyrene cups. This man-made material doesn't conduct heat well, so the drink stays hot and you can hold the cup and not get burned.

People often line their attics with foamy or padded insulating material. This helps trap heat and reduce heating costs.

Everyday materials

All objects are made of at least one material. These pages show the most common materials, which are used to make many of the things you see and use every day.

Glass

Glass is a see-through material that is made when sand melts at a very high temperature. Thin glass, such as in drinking glasses, can be fragile and can break very easily.

Glass is naturally colourless and is used in glasses.

Laminated safety glass in car windows is made by adding clear plastic between layers of glass. This stops it from breaking into sharp pieces.

The coloured glass in marbles is made by adding certain metals to melted glass before it cools.

Metals

Many everyday things are made out of metal. There are lots of types of metals and you can read about the most common ones on pages 54–55.

Wood

Wood is a material that comes from trees. It is hard, strong and heavy and is useful for making furniture and constructing houses.

Wood is tough and long-lasting. Strong saws are used to cut down trees and later to slice the trunks into flat planks.

Paper

Paper is made when wood is mixed with water and chemicals to make a mixture called pulp. The mixture is then spread out into thin layers, pressed flat and allowed to dry.

Paper can absorb ink so it's great for writing, drawing, and printing words and pictures on.

It is flexible and can be dyed different colours or printed with patterns on it, which makes it good for giftwrap.

It can easily be folded, cut and stuck together which means it's perfect for making books.

Find out more about: **absorbing** (page 47); **flexible** (page 49)

Cardboard

Cardboard is thick, stiff paper. It is soft and flexible enough to be cut and folded, so it is widely used to make boxes to contain or protect all kinds of things from matches to furniture.

Thin cardboard is ideal for food packaging, such as cereal boxes.

Thick cardboard is strong enough to protect and carry heavy items when you move house.

Plastic

Plastics are made in factories using chemicals that are found in oil. There are lots of different kinds. Plastics don't carry heat or electricity well which makes them good for making into pan handles and coverings for electrical wire. They have many other useful properties too:

Plastics can be hard and rigid...

They are waterproof.

...or soft and flexible.

They can be moulded into any shape and dyed any colour.

Fabrics

Fabrics are flexible materials made of strands of fibres woven together. They are made into all kinds of things from clothes and sheets to tents and sails. Wool, cotton and canvas are natural fabrics, made of fibres from plants or animals.

Cotton keeps you cool in warm weather so is perfect for T-shirts and sportswear.

Wool keeps you warm when it's chilly so is good for sweaters. It traps your body heat next to your skin.

Canvas is woven cotton, linen or hemp. It is hard-wearing and is often used to make bags and shoes.

Some fabrics, such as nylon and polyester, don't occur naturally but are made in factories.

Nylon is lightweight, waterproof and very flexible so is perfect for umbrellas.

Lycra is stretchy and quick to dry, so it's used to make sportswear and dancers' costumes.

Polyester is soft and dries quickly so it's a good material for making into shower curtains.

Find out more about: **electricity** (page 86); **heat** (page 94)

53

Metals

Metals are shiny, hard, strong materials that come from rocks in the Earth called ores. They can be used on their own, or in a mixture, to make all kinds of everyday objects.

Properties of metals

Here are some of the properties that metals have in common.

All metals conduct electricity well and are ductile so they're perfect for wires in electrical appliances.

They are shiny and hard-wearing. Some metals are used to make coins.

Metals are good at conducting heat, so are suited to making pots and pans for cooking.

Some metals are magnetic which means they attract some other metals to them.

If you hit something made of hollow metal it will make a ringing sound.

Metals are malleable (they can be bent or beaten flat). They are used to make all kinds of vehicles.

Corrosion

Many metals are shiny and sparkly but some can become dull. This is called corrosion or tarnishing and happens when the metals come into contact with air and water.

Gold

Gold is shiny, yellow and attractive. It is seen as rare and valuable so it is known as a precious metal.

Gold is so valuable that many countries keep their riches as gold bars.

Silver

Silver is a shiny, whitish metal that is used to make jewellery and cutlery. It's used in some mirrors and musical instruments.

Silver is a precious metal. It is easy to shape and engrave so it is ideal for jewellery.

Aluminium

Aluminium is a very light, silvery-grey metal. It does not corrode easily.

Aluminium is used to make aircraft, ships and drinks cans.

Lead

Lead is a soft, blue-grey metal. If it's melted, its liquid form is shiny and silvery.

Lead is used in roofing materials, in car batteries and in hospitals and laboratories to shield against x-rays.

Copper

Copper is a soft, orange metal, used in water pipes and electrical wires.

Copper is widely used to make central heating pipes that carry hot water around the house.

Tin

Tin is a light, soft, silvery metal that resists corrosion well. Many metal things are coated in tin to protect them.

Food cans are often made of steel that has been covered in a thin layer of tin to stop it from corroding.

Iron

Iron is a heavy, strong, silvery-grey metal. It is used to make fences, pans, hinges, screws and bolts. When iron is exposed to air and water it forms rust – a gritty reddish substance that weakens the iron.

Once iron is heated up, it holds onto heat energy for a long time, making it a good metal to use for cookware.

Mercury

Mercury is the only pure metal that is a liquid at room temperature. It has a shiny, silvery colour.

Mercury was once widely used in thermometers. As the temperature rises, the mercury liquid expands and moves up the tube.

Mercury

Alloys

An alloy is a mixture of metals. Alloys are useful because they combine properties of the metals in them.

Bronze

Bronze is the oldest man-made alloy, made by melting and mixing copper and tin. It is strong (like copper) and resists corrosion (like tin). When it was invented thousands of years ago it was used for tools and weapons.

Bronze is very tough and can be shaped into cymbals and bells that make a clear, lasting sound.

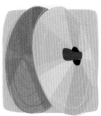

It resists corrosion so is ideal for door knockers and fittings on ships that are exposed to all weathers.

Steel

Steel is an alloy of a metal (iron) and a non-metal (a material called carbon). A small amount of carbon makes the iron super tough.

Steel is used to make things that need to be really strong, such as the frames of skyscrapers.

Find out more about: **expansion** (page 50); **heat** (page 94); **liquids** (page 58)

Disposing and recycling

Throwing away waste or something you've finished using is known as disposing. Using it to make something else is called recycling.

Waste

Waste is anything people no longer need and so throw away. People can reduce waste by using less (for example choosing brands with less packaging), using things again (such as plastic bags) or recycling them.

Household waste includes newspapers, bottles, jars, boxes and left-over food.

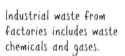

Industrial waste from factories includes waste chemicals and gases.

Biodegradable waste

Biodegradable waste is something that will rot away and can become part of the soil. Organic waste (from plants and animals) and some special plastics are biodegradable.

You can turn organic waste into fertilizer by making a compost heap where the waste can rot.

Carrot seeds

Baby carrots

A compost heap works like this:

Peelings

Compost heap

Recycling

Recycling is making new things from things that have already been used. Something that can be recycled is **recyclable**. Households collect their recyclable materials which are then taken to recycling centres.

Some materials can be made into new versions of the same thing: old newspapers can be turned into paper for new newspapers.

Some materials can be recycled into something completely different. Old cars can become new drinks cans.

Recycling centre

A recycling centre is where collected recyclable materials are brought to be sorted and broken down so they can be made into new things.

This logo means that either something can be recycled or that it is made from recycled material.

People place their recyclable waste in recycling bins, then it's all collected and taken to a recycling centre.

A recycling centre is a huge building in which different materials are sorted and cleaned.

The materials are then crushed, ground up or shredded into smaller pieces so that they can be recycled.

Find out more about: **fertilizer** (page 16)

Energy from waste

One way of making waste work for us, instead of polluting our planet, is to use it to get electricity.

Landfill sites

Landfill sites are places where non-recyclable waste is buried in huge holes in the ground.

Using methane

1. Non-recyclable waste collected from homes is taken to landfill sites, tipped into huge holes and buried.

2. Decaying waste gives off methane gas. This can be collected at landfill sites and burned to give electricity and heat.

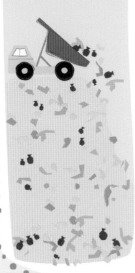

Collection truck

Storage tank

Methane from buried waste collects in pipes.

Incinerator

Incinerators are huge oven-type buildings where waste is destroyed by burning it at high temperatures. Burning waste can produce harmful gases which could spread into the atmosphere and pollute the air. Modern incinerators have equipment to control air pollution.

Using heat

1. When waste is burned in special incinerators the heat can be trapped and used to make steam.

2. The steam is used to drive machines called generators, whose movement generates electricity.

Waste being loaded in incinerator

Water tank producing steam

Fire heating water tank

Littering

Throwing waste away anywhere other than in a bin, or at a dump or waste collection point, is littering. This can harm wildlife and the environment and is illegal in many countries.

Pollution

Pollution is damage to the environment caused by human activities.

Burning waste in incinerators creates harmful gases, but the gases can be cleaned to reduce pollution before being released into the air.

Find out more about: **electricity** (page 86); **methane** (page 65)

Solids, liquids and gases

Materials can be described as solids, liquids or gases. These are called the **states of matter** and each state has its own properties.

Solids

Solids keep their shape well and don't flow or spread out on their own.

Solids always take up the same amount of space. The cut-up pieces of a solid take up as much room as the solid did before it was cut.

Solids, liquids and gases are made up of tiny particles. These are so small they are invisible without the strongest microscopes.

In solids, such as metals, particles sit close together. They move a little but keep in much the same position, so solid materials keep their shape well.

Everyday solids

Wood	Brick
Ice	Cheese
Glass	Wax crayon
Cardboard	
Paper	

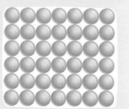

Liquids

Liquids aren't firm: they flow and can be poured easily. They aren't easy to hold – if you try lifting water it will trickle between your fingers.

Liquids change their shape depending on the shape of the container they're in.

Like solids and gases, liquids are made up of tiny invisible particles. In liquids, the particles sit slightly apart from each other and they move a little.

In liquids, such as water, the particles sit slightly apart from each other and they can move around each other. This is why liquids flow and can be poured.

Everyday liquids

Water	Syrup
Perfume	Paint
Hot chocolate	Orangeade
Shampoo	
Cough syrup	

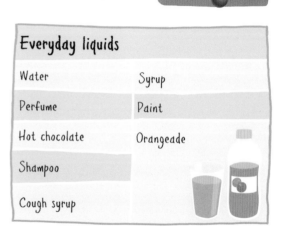

Find out more about: **metals** (page 54)

Gases

A gas has no particular shape and can drift easily from one area to another – for example hot air filling a cold room. Many gases are invisible, but we are showing them as dots to help explain how they behave.

Gases take up as much room as is available and take on the shape of whatever container they are in, such as these jars.

Gases can be squashed into a small space, such as air inside a balloon...

...or they can spread out to fill a huge space – which is why you might smell the scent of roses across a garden.

Like solids and liquids, gases are made up of tiny invisible particles. Particles in gases are far apart from each other and they are very free to move.

The greater distance between the particles in a gas allows gases such as air to spread out into larger spaces or to be squeezed into smaller ones.

Everyday gases

Air	Oxygen
Carbon dioxide	Helium (in balloons)
Steam	Natural gas (used in cooking)
Car exhaust fumes	
Body gases (burps...)	

Volume and shape

Volume is the amount of space something takes up and shape is the form or outline of something. A material's volume and shape depend on its state.

Volume and shape facts

Solids	A solid always has a fixed volume, and it has a definite shape.
Liquids	A liquid has a fixed volume but its shape can change.
Gases	A gas does not have a fixed volume or a definite shape.

Grains and powders

Solids are not all bulky and can also be tiny grains or powders such as sand or cocoa. Grains can sometimes be poured because the individual grains are free to move over each other. But sugar, salt and so on are all described as solids because each grain keeps its shape and you can't pour one grain.

You could pour the sand grains out of this bucket and then press them together to make a bigger solid shape, such as this sandcastle.

Find out more about:
measuring volume (page 116)

Changing state

Some materials stay in one state, as a solid, liquid or gas. Some change from one state to another when they are heated or cooled.

Freezing

When a liquid freezes it turns into a solid. Its temperature drops so low that it can't flow so it stays in one place and its shape becomes fixed.

You can turn liquid fruit juice into a solid ice lolly by putting it in the freezer.

Water freezes at 0°C (32°F) but other materials turn to solids at different temperatures.

Liquid jelly turns into a solid at about 3°C (37°F). It sets in the shape of the container it was in.

Melting

When a solid melts it turns into a liquid. As its temperature gets higher it loses its shape and starts to flow.

As a candle flame heats the solid wax, it turns to liquid.

Out of the freezer, ice cream melts and turns to gloopy liquid.

Evaporation

Evaporation is the change that happens when a liquid turns into a gas. If a liquid heats up enough, the particles inside it spread out until the liquid becomes a gas.

When a dog gets warm, it pants, letting water evaporate from its tongue. Its tongue gets colder and so cools the dog.

Condensation

Condensation is the change that happens when a gas turns into a liquid. It is the opposite of evaporation.

If you breathe onto a cold window, water vapour in your breath cools and condenses to cloud the window with tiny droplets of water.

Sublimation

Sublimation is the change that happens when a material turns from solid to gas (or gas to solid) without becoming a liquid at all. Only a few materials sublime.

"Dry ice" is a material that sublimes. It is used at concerts to produce a foggy effect.

States of water

Water can exist as a solid, liquid or gas, depending on its temperature. You can raise or lower its temperature to watch it change state.

The temperatures at which a material's changes of state happen have different names, depending on which state is changing into which.

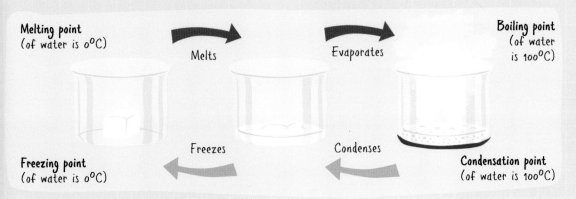

Melting point
(of water is 0°C)

Melts

Evaporates

Boiling point
(of water is 100°C)

Freezes

Condenses

Freezing point
(of water is 0°C)

Condensation point
(of water is 100°C)

The water cycle

The water cycle is the way water moves around the planet by changing state.

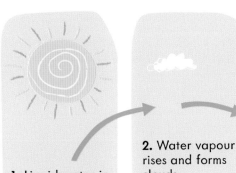

1. Liquid water in seas, oceans and lakes warms up and evaporates to form **water vapour.**

2. Water vapour rises and forms clouds.

3. The water vapour in clouds cools and condenses. When the cloud can hold no more water, it falls as **rain.** If it's cold, water freezes and falls as **ice** or **snow.** (This later melts.)

4. The water drains into rivers which flow into the seas, oceans and lakes and the whole process begins again.

Electrical conductors

Some materials let electricity pass through them easily. These materials are known as electrical conductors.

Conducting metals

All metals, such as copper, iron and steel, are good electrical conductors. This is why the parts of electrical objects that need to let electricity pass through them are always made of metal.

Electricity flows into the metal filament (a thin wire) inside a light bulb and makes it glow.

Metal filament

Metal prong

A metal USB plug conducts electrical computer signals to and from computers.

Inside a USB cable, metal wires conduct electrical signals between computers and other electronic products such as cameras.

Metal wire

Faraday cage

A Faraday cage is a cage made out of metal. If it comes into contact with electricity, the electricity flows around the cage and doesn't affect anything that is inside it. During a lightning storm, a car is the safest place to be because it acts as a Faraday cage if lightning strikes it.

Electric shocks

An electric shock is a burn or nerve injury caused by electricity passing through the body. Electricity is dangerous to living creatures because the water inside them is a good electrical conductor.

Lightning rods

Lightning rods are long metal poles that are used to stop lightning from damaging tall buildings.

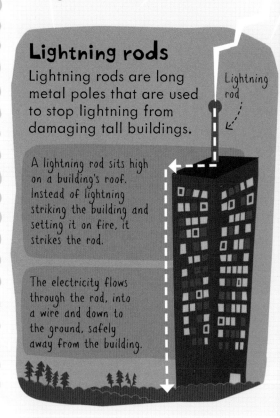

Lightning rod

A lightning rod sits high on a building's roof. Instead of lightning striking the building and setting it on fire, it strikes the rod.

The electricity flows through the rod, into a wire and down to the ground, safely away from the building.

Electrical insulators

Some materials do not allow electricity to pass through them easily. These materials are known as electrical insulators.

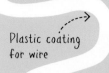

Plastic coating for wire

Plastic is a good electrical insulator. It is used to cover materials that carry electricity, to protect people from electric shocks.

Soil and rocks

The ground is made up of natural materials such as rocks, stones and soil.

Types of rock

Rock is the natural material that mountains are made of. There are many types, some are harder than others. Very soft rock wears away easily. Rocks that are **permeable** let water soak through them. **Impermeable** rocks don't.

Chalk and **gypsum** are soft and permeable. They wear away easily so are great for drawing on blackboards and paving stones.

Limestone is permeable, and can be cut into blocks for building. The Great Pyramid of Giza in Egypt was made from limestone blocks.

Marble is very hard and impermeable. It is used to make grand buildings, statues and other things designed to look good for a long time.

Slate is impermeable. It is used to make roof tiles as it keeps the rain out.

Stones and pebbles

Stones are small rocks. Pebbles are smaller oval or round stones found on beaches. They have been worn smooth by water and sand.

Sand

Sand forms when the action of the sea breaks rock down into tiny grains. It is mostly found on beaches.

In some areas soil is sandy. Sandy soil is pale, and water drains through it easily so it usually feels quite dry.

Soil

Soil is a mixture of tiny pieces of rock, dead plants and animals, water and air. Different soil types offer different growing conditions for plants.

Clay is sticky and is often slightly blue. It has very few air gaps in it, so rain stays on top for a long time.

Chalky soil is light brown. Water drains quickly through it.

Loamy soil is brown and crumbly and easy to dig. It rarely gets too wet or dry, and many types of plants grow well in it.

Air and the atmosphere

Air is a mixture of gases that forms a layer called the atmosphere around the Earth. All living things need air, to breathe or to use to make food.

Air gases

Air contains 21% oxygen and 78% nitrogen. The final 1% of air contains gases such as argon, carbon dioxide, water vapour and some rarer gases.

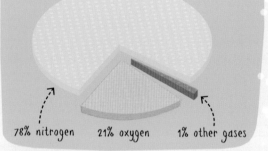

78% nitrogen   21% oxygen   1% other gases

Oxygen

Oxygen is a gas that has no colour or smell. When animals breathe in air, they use the oxygen and breathe out the other gases. There is less oxygen higher up in the atmosphere, so some mountain climbers take oxygen with them in tanks.

Scuba divers carry tanks of oxygen so they can breathe underwater.

Carbon dioxide

Carbon dioxide gas is colourless and has no smell. It is the main waste gas that animals breathe out.

Carbon dioxide

Oxygen

Plants absorb carbon dioxide and use it to make food. They give out oxygen as a waste gas.

Carbon dioxide is used to make the bubbles in fizzy drinks. When you take off the lid they rush to escape.

Carbon dioxide is used in some fire extinguishers. It smothers flames and is safe on burning electrical equipment.

Nitrogen

Nitrogen is a gas that doesn't smell of anything and you can't see it. It is often used in packaging foods such as meat or crisps because it doesn't mix with the food and turn it bad.

Filling packets of food with nitrogen gas helps to keep the food fresh for longer.

Find out more about: **gases** (page 59)

Other gases

These gases are found in smaller amounts than oxygen, nitrogen and carbon dioxide.

Some museums store old documents in cases full of **argon** gas. It stops them from decaying.

Neon is colourless but it glows with an orange-red light when electricity passes through it. It is used to make bright glowing street signs.

Methane burns easily. It is sometimes used as a fuel in power stations.

Air pollution

Air pollution is a build-up of gases such as carbon dioxide, methane and smoke in the air and atmosphere. Small amounts of these gases occur naturally but factories, cars, offices and houses produce larger amounts than the planet can cope with.

Air pollution can damage wildlife, rivers and buildings, and cause breathing difficulties for people.

Smoke carries specks of dirt into the air, but most polluting gases are invisible.

Atmosphere

The atmosphere is a blanket of gases that surrounds the planet. It is made up of layers of different mixtures of gases.

The atmosphere shields the planet from the harmful ultraviolet rays of the Sun. It also traps heat from the Sun's rays close to the surface. This keeps the planet warm enough to support life.

Just the right amount of heat being trapped

Earth's atmosphere

Ozone layer

The ozone layer of the atmosphere contains a gas called ozone. The layer absorbs harmful rays from the Sun but is being damaged by air pollution. In winter and spring a hole forms in the ozone layer at the South Pole, allowing harmful rays through.

Greenhouse gases

Greenhouse gases, such as carbon dioxide and methane, are gases that help to trap some of the Sun's heat near the Earth (in a similar way to glass trapping heat in a greenhouse).

A build-up of greenhouse gases traps too much heat, causing a general rise in the world's temperatures known as **global warming**.

Find out more about: **electricity** (page 86); **pollution** (page 57); **power stations** (page 89)

Mixtures

In science, a mixture is a combination of materials that can easily be separated. It can be any combination of solids, liquids and gases.

Mixing solids

When solids are mixed together, you can often see separate pieces of each solid.

Unmixed solids

Solids mixed together

Mixing liquids

Some liquids mix together completely, while others mix at first but separate when they are left to settle. How well liquids mix depends on how dense (heavy) they are.

Fruit juice and water have very similar densities, so they will stay mixed together.

Oil is less dense than water so it floats to the top after the two have been mixed.

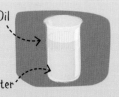

Oil

Water

Solution

A solution is a mixture made when a solid mixes completely (**dissolves**) into a liquid. The solid is known as the **solute** and the liquid is called the **solvent**. A material that dissolves in a liquid is described as **soluble**. One that does not dissolve is **insoluble**. A solution is **saturated** when no more solid can dissolve in it.

Sugar added to fruit juice that is already saturated with sugar sinks to the bottom.

Suspension

A suspension is a mixture of little solid particles floating in a liquid or gas instead of being dissolved in it.

Smoke is a suspension of specks of ash in a mixture of air and other gases.

This muddy water is a suspension of soil, sand and water. If it is left to stand, the solids (soil and sand) settle, forming layers.

Mixed   Settled

Foam

A foam is a mixture of gas bubbles trapped in a liquid or a solid.

Soap lather is a foam of air bubbles in liquid soap.

66 Find out more about: **density** (page 81); **gases** (page 59); **liquids** (page 58); **solids** (page 58)

Separating mixtures

Separating a mixture means dividing it into its original materials. This page shows some methods you can use.

Decanting

When you decant a mixture, you pour away the liquid into another container. You can separate the solid and liquid parts of a suspension or a saturated solution by decanting.

When you carefully pour off the water after cooking pasta, you are decanting a mixture.

Filtering

Filtering a mixture involves pouring it through filter paper in a cone-shaped funnel. This method is good for separating mixtures made up of a liquid and an insoluble solid.

Muddy water

Filter paper

Funnel

Water

If you filter muddy water, the filter paper traps the solid soil and sand but the liquid water trickles through.

Evaporating

You can separate a soluble solid from a solution by heating the solution. The liquid evaporates (it turns to gas) and leaves the solid behind.

You can get the salt out of sea water by boiling the solution. The water evaporates (it turns to steam) leaving the salt behind.

Magnetic separation

Magnetic separation means using a magnet to pick magnetic materials out of non-magnetic materials.

A magnet can separate a mixture of metal paperclips and torn paper. The paperclips are attracted to the magnet; the paper isn't.

Sieving

Sieves are used to separate mixtures of solids that have pieces of different sizes. The parts that are small enough fall through the holes in the sieve, and the larger parts are left behind.

You can use a sieve to separate a mixture of pebbles and sand. The sand falls through the mesh and the pebbles stay in the sieve.

Find out more about: **condensation** (page 60); **evaporation** (page 60); **magnets** (pages 78-79)

Changing materials

As well as being useful on their own, or within mixtures, materials are also interesting and useful because they can change.

Natural changes

Natural changes are changes that happen without anyone making them take place. Many changes occur naturally – a pond freezes during a harsh winter, then melts again when warmer weather comes.

Polar ice drifts happen when sea ice warms up. The solid sheets of ice weaken and break into smaller pieces.

Artificial changes

Artificial changes are changes that involve people. These include cooking and baking. When people mix or heat things, changes can happen.

Mixing together ingredients to make a cake is an artificial change. The ingredients wouldn't mix together by themselves.

Reversible changes

A reversible change is a change that can be undone. Reversible changes are temporary and can easily be switched back, returning the material to its original condition. Mixing solids is a reversible change. This is because the solids can be separated again.

A selection of fruits can be mixed together into a fruit salad. They can be separated out again.

Changing the temperature of something can cause it to change state. This is a reversible change because a material can be returned to its original state by reversing the temperature change.

Chocolate is solid at room temperature.

When it gets warm, it becomes runny as it turns to liquid.

When it cools, the chocolate becomes solid again.

Find out more about: **mixtures** (page 66); **state** (page 58); **temperature** (page 50)

Irreversible changes

An irreversible change is permanent and cannot easily be undone. It forms new materials from the original ones.

Burning something in a fire is an example of an irreversible change. Wood burns to form ash and smoke. The ash and smoke can't be changed back to wood again.

Logs are wood before they are burned...

...and turn into charcoal, smoke and ash afterwards.

After you've cooked some foods, you can't uncook them. They have turned into new types of material, so have been irreversibly changed.

A raw egg can be changed by cooking.

Afterwards, it can't become raw again.

Baking is a process that involves two irreversible changes. Once the ingredients are mixed together, they can't be unmixed. Then, when the batter has been cooked in the oven, it can't go back to being the batter.

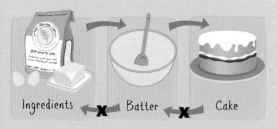

Ingredients   Batter   Cake

Speed of changes

Quick changes happen really, really quickly – in a few seconds or minutes.

The chemicals in fireworks react and explode really quickly once they are set off.

Slow changes happen over a longer time – days, weeks, months or years.

A new material called rust slowly forms on the surface of an iron gate when it is exposed to air and rainwater.

Changes in shape

A material can change shape when a force acts on it (when it is squeezed or stretched). The change might be reversible or not, depending on how stretchy or springy the material is and how great the force is.

There's more on how forces can change the shape of a material on page 80.

Forces in motion

A force is a push or pull. You can't see forces, but you can see how they affect things. A force can make something speed up, slow down or change direction.

Motion

Motion is how something moves. For an object to move, a force has to act on it, so if something is not moving, a force is needed to start it moving.

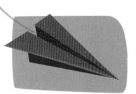 

When you throw a paper plane, your hand applies a force to it to start it moving.

When you kick a still football, your foot applies a force to it to start it moving.

Speed

Speed is how quickly a thing moves. To measure speed, you need to find how far something travels in a certain time. The more force you apply to an object as you make it move, the greater its speed is. Here are some units you can use to measure speed.

metres per second (m/s)	how many metres something travels in a second
kilometres per hour (kph)	how many kilometres something travels in an hour
miles per hour (mph)	how many miles something travels in an hour

You can measure the speed of a racing car in mph or kph.

Balanced force

If two forces are balanced, it means that they are just as strong as each other, but are acting in opposite directions. Balanced forces don't affect the motion of an object.

The two forces here are balanced, so the dog toy is not moving.

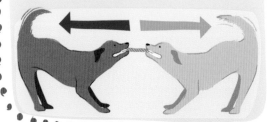

Unbalanced force

If two forces are unbalanced, it means that one is weaker than the other. Unbalanced forces change the motion of an object.

The two forces here are unbalanced – the toy is moving to the left because the dog on the left is pulling with the greater force.

Changing speed

A force is needed to speed something up or slow it down. When something is getting faster it is said to be **accelerating**. When it's slowing down, it is **decelerating**.

As this spacecraft launches, its rockets produce an upward force, making it accelerate upwards.

These skydivers will land safely because their parachutes are applying an upward force as they fall, making them decelerate.

Velocity

Velocity describes how quickly something is moving in a particular direction. It's measured in the same ways as speed with the direction, North, South, East or West added. An object can change velocity by changing direction, accelerating, or decelerating.

This electric toy train is always travelling at the same speed, but its velocity is changing because it is constantly changing direction.

Find out more about: **mass** (page 72)

Momentum

Momentum is a measure of how difficult it is to stop something moving. If something is moving with a lot of momentum, it will take a lot of force to bring it to a stop. How much momentum something has depends on how much mass it has and how quickly it's moving.

Without its brakes on, this heavy truck is rolling quickly. It has a lot of momentum and would need a strong force to stop it.

Heavy truck

Steep hill

This car is lighter than the truck and is rolling slowly, so it has less momentum. It could be stopped by a weaker force than the one needed to stop the truck.

Light car

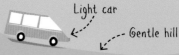

Gentle hill

Twisting

When you twist something, you push and pull it at the same time. This results in a turning motion.

When you twist the lid off a jar, you are pushing one way and pulling the opposite way at the same time to force the lid to turn.

Gravity

Gravity is a force that pulls things together. This pull is because objects have mass. The bigger the mass, the bigger the pull. Only the gravity of really massive objects is noticeable.

The Earth and the Sun both have lots of mass so their pull of gravity is big. Without this pull, the Earth and the Moon would float away into space.

The Earth circles the Sun because of the pull of gravity between the mass of the Earth and the mass of the Sun.

The Moon circles the Earth because of the pull of gravity between the mass of the Moon and the mass of the Earth.

Mass

Mass is the amount of stuff (known as matter) that something contains. It is measured in kilograms. The more mass something has, the bigger its pull of gravity.

Earth's gravity

Earth's gravity is the force that pulls everything on the planet towards the ground. When you drop something, it falls because the Earth has a huge mass, so the effect of gravity is noticeable.

Weight

Weight is the pull downwards on an object because of gravity. It's a force that changes depending on where the object is and how much mass it has.

On the Moon, the pull of gravity is less than it is on Earth, because the Moon has less mass than the Earth. If you went to the Moon, you would weigh $\frac{1}{6}$ of what you weigh now. You wouldn't be any thinner though, so your mass would stay the same.

In space, astronauts get used to feeling light. When they return to Earth, they feel heavy and have difficulty moving normally.

When apples fall from trees, they drop to the ground because of gravity.

Force meter

A force meter (also known as a Newton meter) is a piece of equipment you can use to measure forces. The strength of a force is measured in units called **Newtons**, named after an English scientist, Sir Isaac Newton.

The force of gravity acting on the apple's mass is pulling the scale down on this simple force meter. The meter shows how much the apple weighs in Newtons.

Scientists measure weight in Newtons because weight is a force. One Newton is about the weight of an apple. If you weigh something using other units, such as grams or pounds, you're actually measuring its mass.

Gravitational field

An object's gravitational field is the area where its force of gravity can be felt. Everything in our solar system circles around the Sun as it is within the Sun's gravitational field.

The Sun's gravitational field keeps the planets circling around it.

Centre of gravity

An object's centre of gravity is the point on it where all its weight seems to act. This means that:

• If you push an object up, supporting it directly underneath its centre of gravity, it won't topple over.

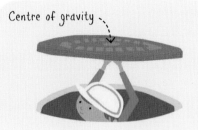

Centre of gravity

• If you pull an object up around its centre of gravity, it's easier to keep it balanced.

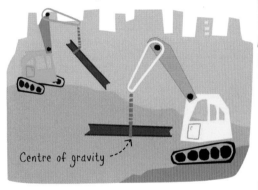

Centre of gravity

• For a spinning object to be balanced, it needs to be spinning around its centre of gravity.

Plate spinning is a skill that involves balancing a spinning plate around its centre of gravity.

Centre of gravity

Find out more about: **acceleration** (page 71); **Sir Isaac Newton** (page 128); **solar system** (page 102)

Friction

Friction is the force between two things that are moving (or trying to move) across each other. The force of friction slows down a moving object.

High and low friction

If there is **low friction** between two things, they'll slide past each other easily. The lower the friction, the longer it will take a moving object to slow down and stop.

These ice skaters can glide along because there's low friction between the blades on the skates and the smooth ice.

If there is **high friction** between two things, they'll rub together and won't be able to slide past each other easily. The higher the friction, the less time it will take for a moving object to slow down and stop.

High friction between the craggy rocks and the rough soles of the climber's shoes is helping this climber to grip the cliff face with her feet.

Air resistance

Air resistance (also called **drag**) is friction between a moving object and the air around it. The air pushes against the object as it gets out of the way to let the object through. This slows the object down unless there's another force to keep pushing it forward.

Sky divers feel air resistance pushing against their face and body as they fall.

This parachute is slowing down the sky diver's fall by providing a large surface for the air to push against.

Heat due to friction

When rough surfaces rub together, friction causes them to get hotter. The rougher the surface and the faster the rubbing, the hotter it becomes.

 Find out more about: **heat** (page 94)

Water resistance

Water resistance is friction between water and an object that is moving through the water. The water pushes against the object as it gets out of the way to let the object through. This slows the object down unless there's another force to keep pushing it forward.

As this frog jumps into a pond, water resistance stops it from hitting the bottom.

Streamlined

If something is streamlined, it means it is smooth and has a sleek shape to reduce the friction caused by it moving through air or water. It doesn't have many rough surfaces or chunks that stick out for the air or water to bump into or rub against.

Dolphins have a streamlined shape.

Smooth surface

Parts that stick out are thin

Lubrication

Lubrication helps to reduce friction between two things by separating them with a thin layer of liquid. For example, putting oil on a bicycle chain helps to reduce the friction between the moving parts.

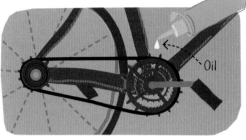

Oil

The oil stays between the moving parts of a bicycle that would rub against each other. This reduces friction so that it takes longer for the metal to wear out.

Friction when rolling

When an object is rolling on a surface, for example a wheel on a road, there is friction between the object and the surface. This slows the object down unless there's another force to keep pushing it forward.

Rolling something along is much easier than sliding it because rolling creates less friction than sliding.

It takes a strong force to slide these heavy bricks...

...but less of a force to roll them.

Pressure

Pressure is force divided by the area it acts on. How much pressure something is under depends on the size of the force and the size of the area the force is pressing down on.

High and low pressure

Increasing a force on an area puts that area under a higher pressure.

Gently tapping this nail with a hammer doesn't have much effect because it only puts the nail under low pressure...

...but hitting the nail hard with the hammer puts it under high pressure, pushing it into the wood.

If a force is spread over a large area, it produces a lower pressure than if the same force was pressing on a small area.

This motorcycle's weight is pressing down on the small area of its thin wheels. This puts high pressure on the soft snow, so the wheels sink into it.

The snow plough has long, wide treads so its weight is spread over a big area. The pressure is less, so the plough doesn't sink into the snow.

Atmospheric pressure

Atmospheric pressure is pressure caused by the weight of the air. The air is made up of tiny particles. Near the ground, the particles are closer together, resulting in more pressure. Higher up, they are further apart, so there is less pressure.

Atmospheric pressure is at its greatest close to the ground and becomes less the higher up you go.

Weather

The weather is what is happening in the atmosphere, so it is affected by atmospheric pressure. If an area has atmospheric pressure that is lower than the places around it, this might bring wind and rain. Areas of high atmospheric pressure are still with clear skies.

When atmospheric pressure drops too low, it can cause storms.

 Find out more about: **atmosphere** (page 64); **particles in gases** (page 59)

Barometer

A barometer is an instrument that measures atmospheric pressure. You can use a barometer to predict what the weather is going to be like.

This barometer measures atmospheric pressure in units called millibars (mbs).

Barometer shows	Weather will be
Slow rise in pressure	Dry
Slow drop in pressure	Rainy and windy
Quick rise in pressure	Fair for a short time
Quick drop in pressure	Stormy

Liquid pressure

Liquid pressure is the force created when a liquid presses down on or against something. The deeper a container of liquid is, the more pressure there is at the bottom.

At the top hole in this juice carton, there isn't much liquid pressure. The juice just trickles out.

There is more liquid pressure at the middle hole. The juice comes out faster and goes further.

At the bottom hole, all the juice above is pushing down, creating the most pressure.

Hydraulic machines

Hydraulic machines are machines that use liquid pressure. A liquid can't be squashed, so if you press one part, pressure increases throughout the whole of it. The only way it can react to this pressure is by moving.

A car's brakes are hydraulic, using liquid pressure.

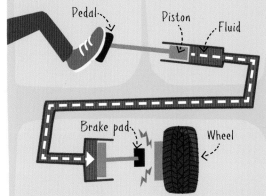

1. The driver pushes a pedal, which pushes a piston.

2. The pressure of the piston forces fluid down a pipe.

Pedal

Piston

Fluid

Brake pad

Wheel

3. The fluid pushes the brake pads against the wheel.

4. The brake pads cause enough friction to slow the wheel down.

Pneumatic machines

Pneumatic machines are machines which use the pressure of a gas – usually air. A gas can be squeezed into a smaller space and this increases the pressure it gives out.

Inside a pneumatic drill, air is under so much pressure that it pushes the metal drill bit with enough force to break concrete.

Find out more about: **friction** (page 74); **gases** (page 59); **liquids** (page 58); **machines** (pages 82-83)

Magnets

A magnet attracts some types of metal towards it by a force called magnetism. It also attracts other magnets. The metals iron, nickel and cobalt can all be made into magnets.

Poles

The ends of magnets are called poles and magnetic forces are strongest here. One end is called the North pole; the other is the South pole.

All magnets have a North and a South pole, no matter what shape they are.

Attraction and repulsion

A magnet's North pole will always pull towards another magnet's South pole. This is described as **magnetic attraction**.

The North and the South poles are pulling towards each other.

Two poles of the same type always push each other away. This is described as **magnetic repulsion**.

The two South poles are pushing away from each other.

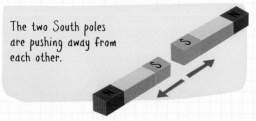

Magnetic materials

A magnetic material is one that is attracted to a magnet. It can only be attracted to a magnet – never repelled by one. The most common magnetic metals are iron, nickel and cobalt. Some materials made with these metals can be attracted to magnets too.

Steel contains iron, so many types of steel, including the type used to make pins and screws, are attracted to magnets.

Non-magnetic materials

Materials that aren't attracted to magnets are described as non-magnetic. Only a few metals can be attracted to magnets; most metals and all other types of materials are non-magnetic.

Tiny pieces of iron and grains of sand

Magnet

Sand   Iron

If you move a magnet slowly over a mixture of iron pieces and sand, the iron will stick to the magnet because it is magnetic and the sand will stay where it is because it's non-magnetic.

Magnetic compass

A magnetic compass is a small magnet balanced on a point, and is used to show which way is magnetic North. Whichever way you turn a compass, the magnet (called a needle) will swing around so that one end is always pointing North. Calling a magnet's pole the North pole is a short way of saying that it is the "North seeking pole".

In this compass, the end of the needle that always points North is painted red.

Geomagnetism

The Earth acts like a giant magnet. There is very hot, liquid iron in the middle of the Earth which some scientists think causes the magnetism. The Earth's magnetism is called geomagnetism.

Although it seems odd, the North pole due to this magnetic effect of the Earth is near the bottom of the planet and the South pole is near the top.

Opposite poles of magnets attract, so North-seeking poles of magnets on the surface of the Earth are attracted to geomagnetic South (inside the Earth).

Magnetic fields

A magnetic field is an area around a magnet where objects can be affected by its magnetic force. You can see the shape of a magnetic field by spreading tiny pieces of iron around a magnet. The pieces form lines known as **magnetic field lines**.

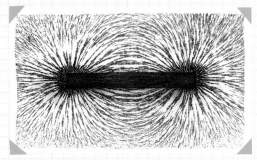

The way the iron pieces are arranged shows the lines of force in the magnet's magnetic field.

Electromagnetism

An electric current flowing through a wire produces a magnetic field around the wire. This is called electromagnetism and makes very powerful magnets. The wire will stop being magnetic when the electric current is switched off.

Huge electromagnets are used in scrapyards to lift cars. The car will drop when the electric current is switched off.

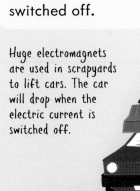

Find out more about: **electric current** (page 86)

Elasticity

An object might change its shape or size when a force acts on it. But if that object has elasticity, it can return to its original form.

Stretching

Stretching is pulling something so it is longer or wider. Stretching an elastic object results in a force that pulls the object back in to its original size and shape when you stop stretching.

Stretched   Normal

Pulling this stretchy elastic waistband will change the shape of the shorts, but they will return to normal when the stretching stops.

Compressing

Compressing is squeezing something so it becomes smaller. Compressing an elastic object results in a force that pushes the object back out to its original size and shape when you stop compressing.

Compressing this bouncy toy changes its shape, but it returns to normal when the compression stops.

Springs and elastic bands

A **spring** is a curly coil of wire. An **elastic band** is a ring of rubber. Both these things have elasticity, which makes them useful in lots of ways.

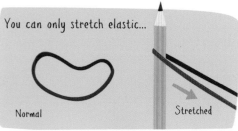

You can only stretch elastic...

Normal   Stretched

...but you can stretch or compress a spring.

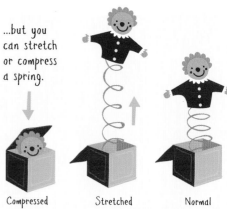

Compressed   Stretched   Normal

Elastic bands are used...	Springs are used...
...to keep loose items together	...to make mattresses and chairs comfortable
...to power wind-up model engines	...to give a smoother ride in cars and bikes
...in toy sling shots	...in clocks and watches
...in dental braces	...in weighing equipment
...in surgical operations	...in switches, such as light switches
...as exercise equipment	...in clickable ballpoint pens

Floating

Some objects can float, which means they rest on water or in air. Other objects sink – they move to the ground or to the bottom of a liquid. Whether something floats or not depends on its shape and what it is made of.

Density

Density describes how many particles are packed into a space and how heavy those particles are.

The particles inside this material are heavy and packed closely together. It is dense.

The particles inside this material are light and spaced further apart. It is less dense.

If something is less dense than water, it could float in water. If it's less dense than air, it could float in air. Two objects can be exactly the same size, but they may have very different densities.

The helium balloon floats because, overall, it's less dense than air.

The ball is the same size as the balloon, but doesn't float because, overall, it's more dense than air.

Displacing and upthrust

When an object is put in water or into the air, the particles of water or air are pushed aside, or **displaced.** You can't see the effect of air being displaced, but you can sometimes see it in water.

Rocks displace water, making the water level rise.

Water or air pushes back against an object placed in it with a force called **upthrust.** If the force of upthrust is the same as the weight of the object, it will float.

Upthrust of water

Weight of boat

Shape and floating

Changing the shape of an object can change whether or not it floats. Modelling clay, for example, can be made into a boat shape, so it contains some air. This makes it less dense than a solid ball of clay.

A solid ball of modelling clay is more dense than water, so it sinks.

Clay made into a boat shape is, overall, less dense than water, so floats.

Find out more about: **particles in solids, liquids and gases** (pages 58-59)

Machines

In science, using a force to move something is described as **work**. A machine is something that makes work easier to do. Here are some examples of simple machines.

Levers

A lever is anything rigid moved around a fixed point called a **fulcrum**. When a force pushes or pulls one of the lever's moving parts, the other part can move with a stronger force. The fulcrum stays still. Levers can help lift or pull things.

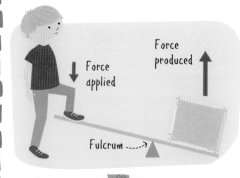

Force applied

Force produced

Fulcrum ------>

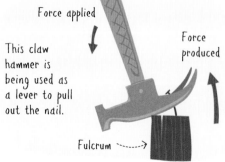

Force applied

Force produced

This claw hammer is being used as a lever to pull out the nail.

Fulcrum ------->

Lots of everyday objects are types of levers. Staplers, nail clippers, fishing rods and even your arms are levers.

Inclined planes

An inclined plane is a sloping surface, such as a ramp. It takes less force to move something up an inclined plane than to lift it straight up.

It's easier to push a heavy box up a slope than to lift it up the same height.

Wedges

A wedge is a solid block of material that is very narrow at one edge and thicker at the opposite edge. Some wedges are used to separate or break things; others are used to stop things from moving.

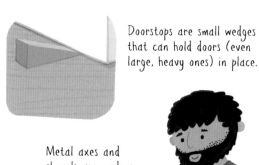

Doorstops are small wedges that can hold doors (even large, heavy ones) in place.

Metal axes and shovels are wedges that separate things.

Pulleys

A simple pulley is a rope around a wheel, used for lifting things. An object is fixed to one end of the rope, and the other end is pulled. As the rope turns the wheel, the object is lifted up. More complicated pulleys have more wheels.

Using a pulley changes the direction of the force and lets you use your body's weight to lift the object up.

Force up

Force down

Wheels

A wheel is any circular frame that turns around a fixed, unmoving point, called a **pivot**. Rolling something on wheels produces less friction than dragging it along the ground. You can find out more about friction when something is rolled on page 75.

Wheels are often connected to rods called **axles**. The force used to turn the wheel is increased by the axle.

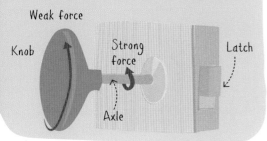

A door knob is actually a kind of wheel. Without a knob, it would take more effort to turn the axle, which moves the latch to open the door.

Weak force

Knob

Strong force

Latch

Axle

Gears

Gears are two or more toothed wheels, called **cogs**, that fit into each other. When one cog turns, it turns the cog next to it in the opposite direction. Gears are used in many machines to change direction. Using gears of different sizes also lets you gain force and change speed.

The larger gears make the smaller ones turn in a different direction at a faster speed.

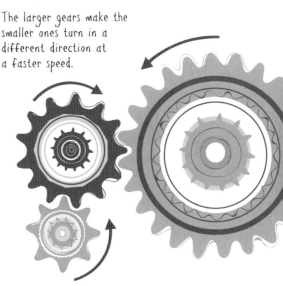

Complex machines

A complex machine is a machine that is made up of two or more simple machines. Some contain many different types.

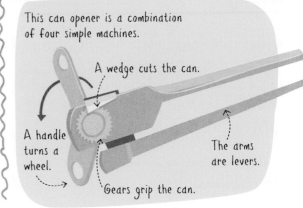

This can opener is a combination of four simple machines.

A wedge cuts the can.

A handle turns a wheel.

The arms are levers.

Gears grip the can.

Energy

Energy is the ability to do work. When things move and when forces act, energy is transferred from one place to another.

Effects of energy

Energy is found in different places, and it is everywhere. You can't always see it, but you can see what it does. Here are some examples of places where you find energy.

Light energy – this is energy from a shining light source. The Sun and the tiniest firefly both have light energy.

Thermal energy – this is another name for heat energy. Hot water has thermal energy.

Electrical energy – electricity is the movement of extremely tiny particles called electrons. Their motion is called electric current.

Sound energy – this is the energy of things vibrating which our ears detect as noises. Whistling vibrates your lips and the air around them.

Gravitational potential energy

Gravitational potential energy is a store of energy something has when it's been lifted up from the ground to a higher place. For example, a book on a bookshelf has gravitational potential energy.

Kinetic energy

Kinetic energy is energy that something has because it is moving.

This skier waiting to ski down the mountain has lots of gravitational potential energy because he is high up the slope.

The skiers whizzing down the slopes have kinetic energy because they are moving.

Chemical potential energy

Chemical potential energy is energy that something has stored inside it. Food, batteries, and fuels such as coal and oil, have chemical potential energy.

A log of wood has chemical potential energy. When the wood burns on a fire, the chemical energy moves from the log to its surroundings to heat and light them up.

When a flashlight is on, chemical potential energy stored in the battery moves from the battery to the surroundings to produce light.

Energy sources

Energy sources are stores of energy. Sources that can't be replaced once they are used up are described as **non-renewable**. **Renewable** sources will not run out.

Fossil fuels

Fossil fuels are non-renewable energy sources, such as coal, oil and natural gas. These formed millions of years ago from the remains of living things. When the fuels burn, chemical potential energy stored inside them moves to the surroundings to produce heat and light.

Oil platforms like this one are used to drill for oil and natural gas that lie under the seabed.

Renewable energy

Renewable energy sources can be replaced, and will not run out. These include kinetic or chemical energies from the natural world.

Hydroelectric power – this is electrical power generated from the movement of water, for example from the flow of a river or the motion of water through a dam. The movement turns machines called turbines, which generate electricity.

Solar power – this is power from solar energy which is heat and light energy from the Sun. It can be stored as chemical potential energy in solar panels or solar cells.

Geothermal power – this is power from natural sources of heat inside the Earth. Rocks deep underground are extremely hot. If water runs over them, it turns into steam and the steam's heat energy can then be used to turn turbines, which generate electricity. Geothermal energy is used in areas with lots of volcanoes.

Biomass power – this is power that comes from burning fuels such as wood, which are made from living things. If new trees are planted to replace those cut down, there will always be wood to burn.

Wind power – this is power from the kinetic energy of moving air. The movement of the wind turns the blades of wind turbines, which generate electricity.

Wind turbines

Electricity

Electricity is the flow of very tiny particles called electrons, that are found in all materials. A battery gives the electrons a push. Metals are materials that have electrons that move very easily, and so the electrons flow through them.

Electric charge

Electrons have something that is called electric charge. Electrons have a negative electric charge. There are positive charges too. Positive and negative charges attract each other. Charges of the same kind push each other away.

Electric current

Electric current is the flow of electrons, which have negative charge. They are pushed around a circuit by a battery or a mains supply.

Electrons move through this circuit because of the mains power supply and so the festive lights glow.

Electrical appliances

An electrical appliance is a machine that works because of electricity.

All sorts of household appliances and electrical gadgets use electricity.

Kettles, ovens, fridges and freezers use electricity to heat and cool things.

Light bulbs and street lamps light up when electricity passes through them.

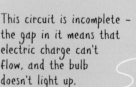
Smartphones use electricity to give out light and sound, and to sort information.

Some cars and trains run on electricity.

Electrical circuits

An electrical circuit is a complete pathway that an electric current can flow around. Current flows when an electric charge moves round a circuit, so a circuit needs a power source and an unbroken path.

This circuit is complete – it has no gaps, so electric charge can flow, and the bulb lights up.

Power supply ----

This circuit is incomplete – the gap in it means that electric charge can't flow, and the bulb doesn't light up.

86 Find out more about: **electrical conductors, electrical insulators, electric shocks** (page 62)

Batteries

A battery is a power source. It is a store of chemical potential energy that can power a circuit. It gives the electrons that are already everywhere in the circuit a push so that they move around the circuit. Batteries run out of power when all their stored energy has been converted and used up.

Terminals – these are the two ends of a power source. The current flows between them.

The positive (+) terminal pulls the negative electrons towards it.

The negative (–) terminal pushes the negative electrons away from it.

Voltage – this is a measure of the strength of the push that a battery gives to the electrons. It's a measure of how powerful the battery is – how much current can flow through a circuit.

1.5V   3V

Voltage is measured in volts (V). The higher the voltage, the more powerful the battery is.

Leads

Leads are lengths of plastic-covered electrical wire with metal connectors at the ends. They are used to complete circuits, connecting components to a power source.

Some leads have connectors called **crocodile clips** that clip onto things to join them together in a circuit.

Components

Components are parts in an electric circuit that do something when electricity flows through them.

Bulbs – these light up when electricity passes through them.

Buzzers – these make a sound when electricity passes through them.

Motors – these move when electricity passes through them. This motor is driving a red fan.

Switches

A switch is part of a circuit that can easily be opened and closed to control the flow of electric current.

This switch is open (off), so there is a gap in the circuit. Electricity can't flow around the circuit to light the bulbs.

On | Off

Switch---↗

This switch is closed (on), so it makes the circuit complete. Current flows around the circuit and the bulbs light up.

On | Off

Find out more about: **chemical potential energy** (page 85); **lightning** (page 62)

Constructing circuits

To build a simple electrical circuit, you need a battery, leads and a component such as a bulb.

A simple circuit with a bulb

You can change components or add extra ones to see what happens in more complicated circuits. For example, two bulbs in a circuit like the one below shine more dimly than one bulb would. Using a wire that was very much longer would make the bulbs even dimmer.

A circuit with two bulbs

A battery with a higher voltage increases the current in the circuit to make the bulbs shine more brightly.

A circuit with a more powerful battery

You might also add switches into a circuit to control the current, switching it on and off.

Circuit diagrams

Circuit diagrams are drawings of electrical circuits that use symbols to represent the power source and circuit components.

Here are some useful symbols that stand for different things you might find in a circuit:

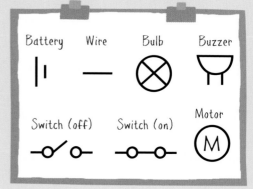

Battery   Wire   Bulb   Buzzer

Switch (off)   Switch (on)   Motor

This simple circuit diagram shows a single battery and a bulb.

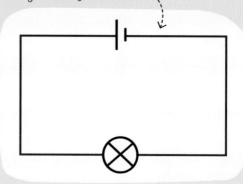

This diagram shows a battery, a switch and two bulbs. The switch is open so there is not a complete circuit. The current can't flow, so the bulbs don't light.

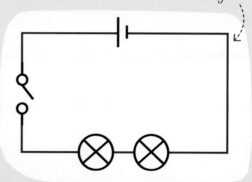

Static electricity

Static electricity (or just "static") occurs naturally. Things can become charged by rubbing them – because of friction. Static often builds up on the surface of electrical insulators such as rubber or plastic.

Rubbing a balloon on clothing builds up a negative charge on the balloon. If you hold it against a wall, it will attract positive charges to it, and cling to the wall.

If you touch a material that has been charged up in this way, you may feel a small electric shock. If someone has been scuffing their feet on a nylon carpet and then touches you, this can happen. The static electricity flows (discharges) through you to the ground.

Lightning

Lightning is a spectacular natural example of static electricity being discharged. During a storm, electric charge can build up at the bottom of some clouds. A cloud loses this static charge by sending a bolt of lightning to another cloud or to the ground below.

During lightning storms, tall buildings are more likely to be struck as they are closest to the discharging clouds.

Power stations

Power stations generate electricity. Heat is used to make electricity, which can then be used to power things.

1. A tank of boiling water produces steam.

2. The steam is used to drive fans called turbines.

3. The moving turbines generate electricity.

4. A transformer controls the speed at which the electricity is carried away from the power station.

Pylon

5. The electricity flows through wires (supported by pylons) to homes, offices, factories, hospitals and schools where it powers machines and appliances.

Find out more about: **electric charge** (page 86); **friction** (pages 74-75)

Light

Light is a transfer of energy and it travels in straight lines. Without light you wouldn't be able to see anything.

Light sources

A source of light is something that gives off light when it is heated or burned, or when chemicals inside it react with each other.

Sunlight is the light produced by the Sun as it burns. The Sun is a massive ball of burning gas.

A candle is a solid block of wax with a string wick in it. When it is lit, the flame burns at about 1,000°C (1,832°F) and shines with a warm yellow light.

Some lightbulbs contain wires that glow if they're heated by electricity. Others contain gases that glow when electricity flows through them.

Bioluminescence is a living thing's ability to produce its own light. Some types of animals, such as squid and fireflies, do this when chemicals inside their bodies react with each other.

Fireflies glow to attract mates.

Seeing things

You can see things because light shines out from a light source, bounces off objects, and then enters your eyes. Your eyes collect this information and send it to the brain, which understands it as pictures.

This boy is seeing the flowers because sunlight is bouncing off them and entering his eyes.

Reflecting

Reflecting means bouncing off. Light reflects off a surface at the same angle as it hits it. Surfaces that are smooth and shiny reflect light well, for example mirrors and polished metals. They are not sources of light, but reflect light that shines on them.

Light is hitting this mirror and bouncing straight back off its smooth, shiny surface so the boy can see his reflection.

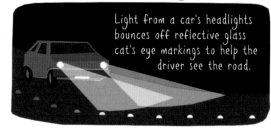

Light from a car's headlights bounces off reflective glass cat's eye markings to help the driver see the road.

Find out more about: **electricity** (pages 86-89)

Transparent

Transparent materials let light pass through them, so you can see clearly what is on the other side.

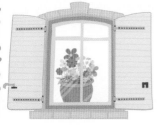

Light is shining straight through this window, giving a clear view of the flowery plant behind it.

Translucent

Translucent materials let some light through, but they scatter it in all directions, and you can't see clearly through them. Translucent objects blur the detail of what you can see.

The light is sent in different directions by this frosted glass, so the view of the flowers on the other side is blurred.

Opaque

Opaque materials block light so it can't pass through. This means you can't see through them.

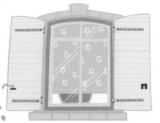

The blind is opaque so you can't see the flowers sitting in the pot behind it.

Speed of light

Light is the fastest moving thing in the universe. It travels about 300,000,000 metres (984,000,000 feet) in one second.

Shadows

A shadow is a dark shape where light doesn't shine. It is made when an opaque object blocks light. The size and shape of a shadow depends on the position of the light source and how far the object is from it.

A tree makes a long shadow at the beginning and end of the day, when the Sun is lowest in the sky.

A tree makes a short shadow at midday, when the Sun is highest in the sky.

Moving an object further away from a light source creates a smaller shadow. Moving it closer to the light source creates a bigger shadow.

This butterfly shape is a long way from the flashlight so its shadow is small.

This butterfly shape is closer to the flashlight so its shadow is bigger.

Visible light

Visible light is light that you can see. It is also described as **white light**, but in fact, it is made up of seven different colours of light – red, orange, yellow, green, blue, indigo and violet.

Visible light spectrum

The visible light spectrum is the group of colours – red, orange, yellow, green, blue, indigo and violet – that make up white light.

Splitting light

When you shine white light through a triangular block of glass called a prism, the light splits into separate colours. The colours separate because each colour slows down and changes direction by a different amount when it travels through the glass.

The change of direction is called **refraction** and the splitting up is called **dispersion**.

As it passes through the prism, violet light bends the most and red light bends the least.

Rainbows

Rainbows happen when beams of sunlight hit water droplets in the air. As the sunlight passes through the droplets it is split into different colours.

Water droplets in a rainbow work like little prisms, splitting white light into wide curves of colours.

Sky colours

The colour of the sky is a result of sunlight hitting dust particles in the atmosphere. The bluey colours bounce and bend in all directions. Some of this light reaches our eyes, making the sky look blue. Other colours don't scatter, and we don't see them.

When the Sun is low in the sky, light has to travel further through more atmosphere to reach your eyes. By the time the light reaches you, the green, blue and violet light has scattered away, leaving only the redder colours.

This dramatic sunset is created because only the orange and red colours reach your eyes.

Absorbing light

Objects can take in, or absorb, light energy. The colour that an object appears to be depends on the colours of light that it can absorb and the colours it reflects (they bounce back).

This leaf is absorbing all colours of light apart from green. Green light is reflecting off its surface and into your eyes.

You see an object as white if it absorbs none of the colours so they all reflect into your eyes.

You see an object as black if it absorbs all colours of light and reflects none.

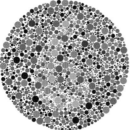

Colour blindness

Some people have a condition known as colour blindness. Their eyes or brain interpret the colours in light differently from other peoples' so they can't see the difference between certain colours.

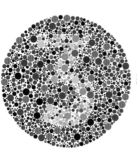

A person who is colour blind may not be able to see the numbers in these patterns.

Ultra-violet light

Ultra-violet (UV) light is a powerful type of energy found in sunshine. It is invisible to humans but you can see its effects when sunshine turns people's skin brown. Too much UV light can lead to skin cancer.

Staying in the shade, using sunscreen and wearing sunglasses, all help to block out UV rays.

Infra-red light

Infra-red is a type of light produced by warm things. Even at normal body temperature a person gives out rays of infra-red light but these are invisible to the naked eye.

Rescue workers use infra-red cameras to find people trapped in collapsed buildings. The cameras detect heat from survivors.

X-rays

X-rays are invisible rays with more energy than UV light. They can pass through some materials but are blocked by others, such as bones and metal.

X-ray machines are used in airports to give views like this that show up metal items in luggage. They are also used in hospitals to see the bones inside people's bodies.

Heat

Heat or thermal energy is the energy something has because of how hot it is and how much of it there is.

Comparing energy

To compare the thermal energies of two objects, you need to think about their size and temperature. Something very hot has a lot of thermal energy. But something that is just warm can have even more if it is very big.

Steaming hot tea is at a higher temperature than a warm swimming pool...

...but the pool has more thermal energy than the tea because there is a lot of water in the pool and only a very little in the mug.

You can increase the thermal energy of an object by doing work on it. For example, rubbing your hands together makes them hotter. Placing an object near a hotter object can increase its thermal energy too.

Holding a cold marshmallow over a flame increases the thermal energy of the marshmallow.

Thermometers

A thermometer is a piece of scientific equipment that measures temperature.

Some thermometers show temperature on a scale of lines with numbers on.

Digital thermometers show the temperature as a number reading.

Celsius and Fahrenheit

Temperature is measured in degrees Celsius or degrees Fahrenheit.

On the Celsius scale	On the Fahrenheit scale
Water boils at 100°C	Water boils at 212°F
Water freezes at 0°C	Water freezes at 32°F
−40°C = −40°F	−40°F = −40°C

°C: 100° 80° 60° 40° 20° 0° −20° −40°

°F: 200° 180° 160° 140° 120° 100° 80° 60° 40° 20° 0° −20° −40°

Absorbing heat

Dark objects absorb more heat than things that are pale, bright or shiny.

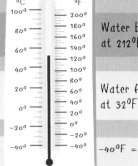

Sports players often wear pale clothes to help them stay cool.

Solar panels are black to absorb as much of the Sun's heat as possible.

Find out more about: **temperature** (page 50)

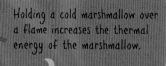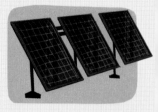

How heat moves

Heat can move from one area to another. It always moves from something hotter to something cooler. There are three ways heat can move.

Conduction – this is how heat moves through an object, or between objects that are touching.

If you leave a cold spoon in a bowl of hot soup, the spoon will get hot because of conduction.

Convection – this is how heat is transferred in a liquid or a gas. The hot liquid or gas spreads out. The cold liquid or gas moves closer to the heat source, warms up and spreads away.

Water at the bottom of a pan warms up and spreads out. It is replaced by more cold water, until all the water is hot.

Air above a radiator warms up and rises. As it cools, it sinks and is sucked closer to the radiator where it heats up again.

Radiation – this is the way that heat moves as invisible waves. Radiation can travel through anything, even empty space. If you warm your hands by a fire, the heat moves by radiation.

The hotter something is, the more heat it radiates. Heat from the Sun travels all the way to the Earth by radiation.

Thermoregulation

Humans and most animals can thermoregulate. This means they can keep their body temperature steady even when the temperature of their surroundings is very different. Human body temperature is about 37°C (99°F).

On a cold night, people will shiver to keep warm. Goosebumps form, which help trap body heat close to the skin to regulate temperature.

When it is hot, people will sweat. As the sweat evaporates the skin cools down and body temperature stays constant.

Hypothermia and hyperthermia

Hypothermia is a medical condition that develops when a person's temperature falls below 35°C (95°F). At such low temperatures the body's organs stop working properly.

Mountaineers and polar explorers have to wrap up warm to avoid developing hypothermia.

Hyperthermia happens when a person's temperature rises above 38°C (100°F). In mild cases, this causes heat stroke – someone faints in the sunshine. In more severe cases, organs fail to work properly.

95

Find out more about: **thermal conductors** (page 51)

Sound

We hear noises because of sound energy. Sound travels in invisible waves.

Vibrations

A vibration is a rapid, repeated movement. Sounds are made when objects vibrate.

Vibrations that cause sounds are often invisible, but if you touch a sound source, such as a loudspeaker, you might be able to feel them.

Sound waves

When something makes a sound, it vibrates and makes the air in and around it vibrate. The vibrating air particles bump into each other, a little like falling dominoes, and so the vibration (the sound wave) travels through the air. When it reaches your ear, you detect the sound.

Sound waves enter the dancer's ears, causing vibrations inside. Her brain interprets them as sounds so she can hear the music.

Medium

A medium is the name given to the material that sound travels through. Sound can travel through different materials, whether they are solids, liquids or gases.

Whales can communicate across large distances because sound waves travel well through the water.

Sound waves travel fastest through solid materials, such as the string in this string and pot telephone.

Vacuum

A vacuum is a totally empty space. It doesn't even contain air. If there is a vacuum between a vibrating object and your ears, you won't be able to hear it, because sound can't travel through a vacuum.

Outer space is a vacuum. A rocket taking off makes a very loud noise on Earth, but you wouldn't be able to hear it passing by you in space.

Volume

The volume of a sound is how loud or quiet it is. For example, plucking a guitar string strongly makes a loud sound. Plucking it gently makes a quiet sound.

Decibel

The volume of a sound is measured in units called decibels. The symbol dB stands for decibels.

The volume of a plane taking off is about 140dB.

The volume of thunder can be about 110dB.

The volume of a motorcycle is about 90dB.

The volume of your regular speaking voice is about 60dB.

Pitch

The pitch of a sound is how high or low it is. A high sound has a high pitch and a low sound has a low pitch. A tight drum skin gives a higher-pitched sound than a loose drum skin.

Frequency

The waves produced when something vibrates very quickly are called high frequency sound waves. Something vibrating more slowly produces lower frequency sound waves.

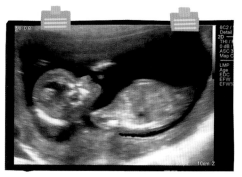

MIAOW

RRRAHR

High frequency waves make high-pitched, squeaky noises.

Low frequency waves make low-pitched, rumbly noises.

Ultrasound

Ultrasound is a vibration with a frequency so high that humans can't hear it.

Ultrasound waves are used to see an unborn baby inside its mother's body. The waves bounce off the baby, creating a signal that forms an image on a computer screen.

Echoes

Echoes are reflected sound waves. If you shout in a big, empty room, the sound of your voice will bounce off the walls and travel back to you.

An echo is a sound reflection.

Find out more about: **reflection of light** (page 90)

Music

Sounds can be arranged to create combinations of higher and lower, longer and shorter, sounds that people want to listen to. This is music.

Musical notes

Musical notes are the sounds that make up music. Notes range from low to high depending on the frequency of their sound waves.

Notes are named with letters A to G that repeat from the lowest notes to the highest ones. All the notes that have the same names, for example all the As, sound similar. They are lower and higher versions of the same note.

Musical instruments

Musical instruments are objects that produce musical notes when people make them vibrate. Making different areas of an instrument vibrate causes different notes. Each type of instrument makes sounds in its own way.

Pianos have a row of 88 keys like these. Pressing a key makes a hammer inside the piano hit three strings. The strings vibrate and make a sound.

C D E F G A B C

Tuning

Instruments need to be tuned so they play at the correct pitch. If the pitch of a note is too high, it is described as sharp. If it's too low, it is flat. String instruments such as guitars can be tuned by turning tuning pegs.

Turning a peg one way shortens the string and makes the pitch sharper.

Turning it the other way lengthens the string, flattening the pitch.

Strings

Tuning pegs

Harmonics

If one part of an instrument vibrates twice as fast as another part, it makes sounds that go well with each other. These pleasing sounds are called harmonics.

Resonance

Resonance happens when a sound echoes around inside an instrument and grows louder.

When you hit a drum, the sound waves spread into the hollow part of the drum and the sound resonates.

Woodwind instruments

Woodwind instruments make sounds when a player blows into them and the air inside the tube vibrates.

Players use their fingers to open and shut holes. Closing holes makes more tube available for the air to vibrate along, which makes lower notes.

Air goes in

Finger holes

Recorder   Clarinet   Saxophone

Brass instruments

Brass instruments make sounds when players blow into them, vibrating their lips against a cup-shaped mouthpiece. The column of air in the instrument vibrates and makes a sound.

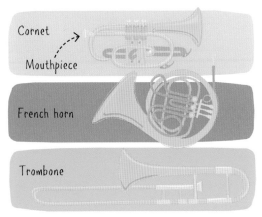

Cornet

Mouthpiece

French horn

Trombone

Players change notes by moving their lips, and pressing valves to let air into extra lengths of tube.

String instruments

A string instrument produces a sound when its strings are plucked or struck, or if a bow slides over them.

Harp

A player slides a bow across the violin strings to make a sound, and presses the strings in different places to change the notes.

A player plucks the strings on a harp to make a sound. Shorter strings make higher notes; longer strings make lower notes.

Percussion instruments

A percussion instrument makes a sound when you hit, shake or scrape it.

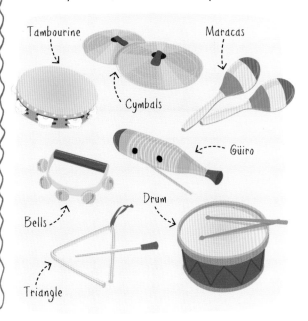

Tambourine

Maracas

Cymbals

Güiro

Bells

Drum

Triangle

Our universe

Our universe is made up of everything we know exists, including stars, planets and moons. There may be other universes out there too, but no one has come up with a way to see them yet.

Light years

Our universe is so huge that distances are hard to imagine if you use normal measurements. Experts use units called light years to describe distances in space. One light year is the distance that light travels in one year. That's 9.46 trillion kilometres or 5.88 trillion miles.

Galaxies

Our universe contains billions of stars, and dust and gas gathered together in huge collections called galaxies. Each galaxy is held together by the force of gravity. Galaxies can be different shapes:

Elliptical galaxies can vary in shape from round to oval.

Spiral galaxies have a bright middle and curved arms of stars.

Barred spiral galaxies have a bar of stars in the middle with an arm at each end.

The Milky Way

The Earth is part of a galaxy called the Milky Way. It is a barred spiral galaxy made up of around 300 billion stars. It measures roughly 100,000 light years across. Like all galaxies, the Milky Way is slowly rotating.

The Earth is here in the Milky Way, about 28,000 light years from the middle.

Stars

A star is a massive ball of hot gas which burns for billions of years, giving off heat and light. The star closest to us is the Sun, which is yellow. Other stars can look white, blue, orange or red.

White or blue stars are usually very bright and are the hottest types of star.

Yellow stars are usually cooler than white or blue stars.

Orange and red stars are cooler and fainter than the other types of star. Some of the biggest stars are red.

Nebulae

Nebulae are massive, swirling clouds of dust and gas where stars are formed. Over tens of thousands of years, due to gravity, the dust and gases clump together. The clumps get hotter and hotter until the gas starts to explode and the middles of the clumps begin to shine. These are stars.

Columns of dust and gas in a nebula

Red giants and white dwarfs

When a star the size of our Sun starts to die (when the supply of gas inside it runs out) it swells up and turns red. At this stage of its life, it's called a red giant. It then loses its outer layers and turns white.

1. A dying star swells into a red giant.

2. The gas on the outside burns away.

3. A heavy, smaller white dwarf is left.

4. The white dwarf cools and fades.

Supernovas

When stars much bigger than our Sun die, they collapse in on themselves, swell up, then explode. These explosions are called supernovas.

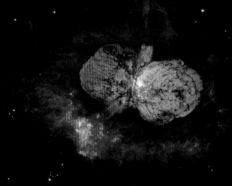

This unstable star may explode in a supernova at any time, giving out as much energy as the Sun will give out throughout its entire life.

Black holes

After the very biggest stars explode, the material that is left collapses in on itself to make an extremely dense object. This is called a black hole. It collapses with such force that it pulls in everything around it, like a giant vacuum cleaner in space.

Black holes look black because they pull in light, but their force makes gas around them shine.

Find out more about: **density** (page 81); **gas** (page 59)

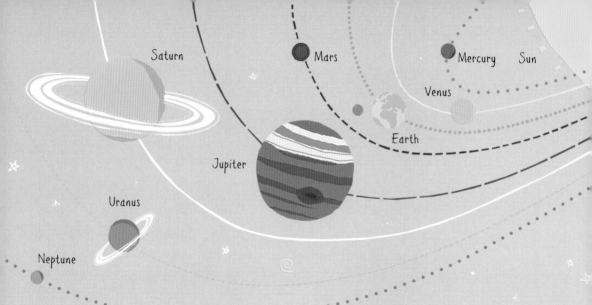

Saturn

Mars

Mercury

Sun

Venus

Earth

Jupiter

Uranus

Neptune

Solar system

A solar system is a star and everything that revolves around it. In our solar system, the star is the Sun. Also in our solar system are eight planets (Mercury, Venus, Earth, Mars, Jupiter, Saturn, Uranus and Neptune), all their moons, and all the lumps of rock, metal and ice moving around the Sun.

Orbit

Orbiting means moving around a point in space. Planets orbit the Sun, and the Moon orbits the Earth. The path they take as they move around is called an orbit too and it is an oval shape.

The dotted line shows the path that the Moon takes as it orbits the Earth.

Planets

A planet is a very large ball of rock or gas that orbits a star, reflecting the star's light. Planets have their own gravity and this force pulls them into a ball shape called a sphere.

Gravity pulls planets into a sphere shape – the most compact shape they can be.

Moons

A moon is a huge lump of rock that orbits a planet. Most moons are rounded. A planet can have more than one moon. You can find out more about Earth's moon on pages 106–107.

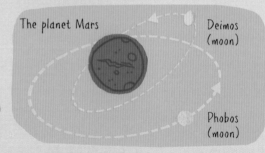

The planet Mars

Deimos (moon)

Phobos (moon)

Asteroids

Asteroids are big lumps of rock or metal that orbit the Sun. They are too big to be meteoroids but too small to be planets. The largest asteroid is around 975km (605 miles) across. Some of the biggest are even orbited by their own little moons.

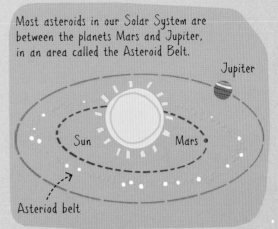

Most asteroids in our Solar System are between the planets Mars and Jupiter, in an area called the Asteroid Belt.

Jupiter

Sun

Mars

Asteriod belt

Meteoroids

Meteoroids are pieces of rock that orbit the Sun. They range in size from tiny grains to huge boulders. Meteoroids sometimes fly so close to the Earth that they are sucked towards it by its gravity.

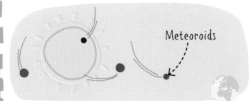

Meteoroids

Meteors

A meteor is a meteoroid that has entered the Earth's atmosphere. Small meteors burn up before they land on Earth. As they burn, they glow brightly. They are also known as shooting stars.

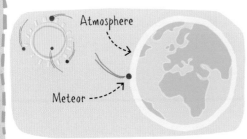

Atmosphere

Meteor

Comets

Comets are lumps of ice, dust and grit that orbit the Sun. As one gets close to the Sun, the heat melts some of its ice and it releases gases and dust. This streams out behind, creating a long tail. Comets sometimes get close enough to the Earth for us to see in the night sky.

A comet called Halley's Comet is visible from Earth every 75 to 76 years.

Meteorites

Meteors that land on the Earth's surface are called meteorites.

Meteorite

Find out more about: **Earth's atmosphere** (pages 64-65)

The Earth and Sun

The Sun is Earth's closest star. Without its heat and light, life on Earth couldn't exist. We also use the Sun to measure time.

Years

A year is the time it takes for a planet to travel all the way around the Sun. On Earth, a year is 365.26 days long, but on Neptune, a year lasts 60,190 days.

The time it takes for the Earth to complete a lap around the Sun is called a **solar year**.

Night and day

It takes 24 hours for the Earth to spin once around its axis. For the side of the Earth that's facing the Sun, the sky is light and it's daytime. When that side is turned away from the Sun, it's night.

Night-time here

Daytime here

Summer here

The Earth is slightly tilted, so its axis slants a little.

Winter here

The Earth's axis

An axis is an imaginary straight line through the middle of an object. The Earth's axis runs from the North Pole to the South Pole. The planet spins on its axis, like a spinning top, turning in an anti-clockwise direction.

Seasons

The Earth is tilted, so there is always a part that is slanted towards the Sun. As the Earth travels around the Sun, the most direct sunlight falls on different areas. This is what gives us the four seasons. Each season has its own type of weather patterns and number of daylight hours.

In the part of the world that is...	The season is...
...tilted to the Sun	...summer
...tilting away from the Sun	...autumn
...tilted from the Sun	...winter
...tilting towards the Sun	...spring

Sunrise and sunset

As the Earth spins on its axis, the Sun seems to rise and set. Earth makes one turn every 24 hours. As it rotates, different places on Earth pass through the Sun's light.

When you're seeing **sunrise**, the place where you are is turning towards the Sun. The Sun is in the East and seems to be rising over the horizon (where the Earth's surface and the sky appear to meet). At **sunset**, your area is leaving the Sun's light, and the Sun appears to be sinking below the horizon in the West.

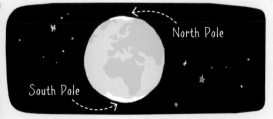

Sunrise

Midday

Sunset

The North and South Poles

The North Pole is the most northern point of the Earth's axis and the South Pole is the most southern point.

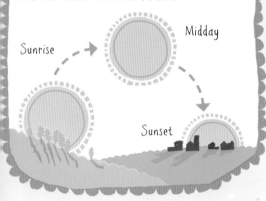

North Pole

South Pole

The poles are permanently cool because the Sun is always low in the sky there in the summer and the Sun's rays do not reach the poles at all in the winter.

Equator

The Equator is an imaginary line around the middle of the Earth that is an equal distance from the North and South poles.

This is where the Equator lies across different parts of the world.

Areas near the Equator are less affected by the changing seasons than the north or the south. This is because each day the Sun strikes at about the same angle, giving about 12 hours of sunlight.

Solar eclipse

Sometimes the Moon passes between the Earth and the Sun, blocking the Sun's light. This is called a solar eclipse. The Moon can cover the Sun because although it is much smaller, it is also much closer to us.

Earth   Moon

Sun

This is what a solar eclipse looks like from Earth as the Moon moves between the Earth and the Sun.

The Moon

The Moon is a dusty ball of rock about 3,476km (2,160 miles) across – a quarter the size of the Earth. It is boiling by day and freezing at night. So far, the Moon is the only part of the Solar System that people have visited.

Phases of the Moon

The Moon doesn't give out any light of its own, but looks bright because it reflects the Sun's light. As it orbits Earth, the amount of the sunlit side we can see varies. This makes it look as if the Moon changes shape every day. The Moon's different shapes are called phases.

Here are the phases the Moon goes through as it completes one orbit of the Earth:

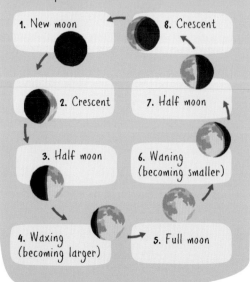

1. New moon
8. Crescent
2. Crescent
7. Half moon
3. Half moon
6. Waning (becoming smaller)
4. Waxing (becoming larger)
5. Full moon

Craters and seas

The Moon has had space rocks crashing into it, making oval holes, called **craters**, in its surface. The surface also has **seas** – dark patches of melted rock (now solid) that flowed out when volcanoes on the Moon erupted billions of years ago.

Sea

Crater

The far side of the Moon

The Moon takes 28 days to spin around once, and 28 days to orbit the Earth too. This means that the same side of the Moon always faces Earth. The other side is called the far side. It has only been seen by space probes and astronauts.

The Luna 3 probe was the first to take pictures of the Moon's far side, in 1959.

 Find out more about: **orbit** (page 102); **reflection** (page 90); **Solar System** (page 102); **space probe** (page 109)

Tides

The Moon is held in orbit by the Earth's gravity, but the pull of the Moon's gravity also affects the Earth. As the Moon orbits Earth, its pull makes the sea level in the oceans rise and fall. The changing sea level is called the tide.

Pull of Moon

The force due to gravity here isn't enough to hold the water in tightly as the Earth moves.

Sea level rises when it is being pulled towards the Moon.

Lunar gravity

Lunar gravity is the force of gravity on the Moon. It is $\frac{1}{6}$ of the force of gravity on Earth. This means that you would be able to jump six times higher or throw a ball six times further on the Moon than you could do on Earth.

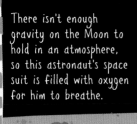

There isn't enough gravity on the Moon to hold in an atmosphere, so this astronaut's space suit is filled with oxygen for him to breathe.

If you tried to walk taking normal steps on the Moon, you would fly too far up into the air and fall over. To avoid this, astronauts do a hopping run to move across the surface of the Moon.

Lunar eclipses

During a lunar eclipse, the Earth passes between the Sun and the Moon, blocking the Sun's light. We see the Earth's shadow creep across the surface of the Moon.

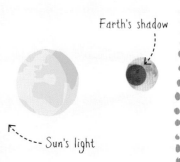

Earth's shadow

Sun's light

A **total eclipse** is when the whole of the Moon enters the darkest part of Earth's shadow. A **partial eclipse** is when only part of the Moon enters the darkest part of Earth's shadow.

No sunlight reaches the Moon during a total eclipse.

During an eclipse, the Moon's colour can appear to change from milky white to brown, red or orange. The shade depends on the amount of dust and cloud in Earth's atmosphere.

Find out more about: **Earth's atmosphere** (pages 64-65); **gravity** (pages 72-73)

Space exploration

Studying space can be as easy as looking at the night sky, but seeing more detail requires special equipment. Astronomers – scientists who study space – use complicated technology to learn about the universe.

Telescopes

A telescope is an instrument that people use to look at distant objects. Telescopes make the objects look bigger and closer.

Optical telescopes make distant objects look bigger by using mirrors, or curved pieces of glass called lenses. Astronomers keep very large, powerful optical telescopes in buildings called observatories.

The simplest optical telescopes are small enough to use pointing out of a bedroom window.

The biggest optical telescopes stand over eight storeys high.

Radio telescopes use dishes to pick up signals, called radio waves, that are given off naturally by space objects. The signals are fed into computers, which turn them into pictures.

1. Radio waves come in.

2. The signals are sent to computers.

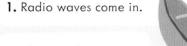

Large dish

3. The computers turn them into images.

Satellite telescopes are big telescopes that have been launched into space to orbit the Earth. Telescopes in space can see much further than those on Earth because they are outside the Earth's atmosphere.

Satellite telescopes are powered by solar panels that collect energy from the Sun.

Space probe Pioneer 11 was the first probe to study Saturn, in 1979.

Space probes

Space probes visit other planets to take pictures of them. All the planets in our Solar System have been visited by space probes. Some just fly close to the planets, some orbit them, and others carry smaller probes that they drop onto the planets.

Space shuttles and Soyuz spacecraft

A **space shuttle** was a reusable spacecraft that carried people and scientific equipment into space. The last shuttle was launched in 2011.

Currently, people are carried into space in **Soyuz spacecraft.** These are capsules that launch attached to rockets.

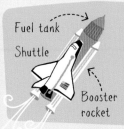

Fuel tank

Shuttle

Booster rocket

After launch, a space shuttle's booster rockets parachuted back to Earth and its fuel tank fell away. The shuttle glided back to Earth when its mission was over.

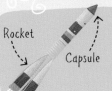

Rocket

Capsule

After launch, a Soyuz spacecraft's rocket falls away and burns up. The capsule parachutes back to Earth when its mission is over.

Rovers

A rover is a small robot on wheels that travels over the surface of a planet or a moon collecting information and taking photographs. It's controlled by astronomers on Earth or on a nearby spacecraft, who send it instructions using computers.

Rovers have cameras to record images, and arms to collect soil and rock samples.

Space stations

A space station is a laboratory in space where scientists carry out experiments that can't be done on Earth. The scientists can live on a station for long stretches of time, sometimes for over a year.

Space stations house living quarters as well as laboratories.

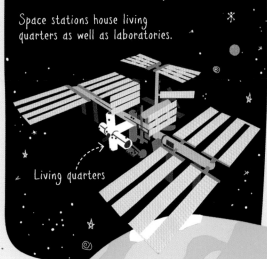

Living quarters

Find out more about: **axis** (page 104); **orbit** (page 102)

Scientific enquiry

You can find out how something works by asking questions about it, and trying to investigate it in a step-by-step process. This is called scientific enquiry or scientific investigation.

Data

Data is another name for information. You collect data when you carry out a scientific enquiry.

Primary sources

A primary source is data you have collected yourself by scientific investigations.

Secondary sources

A secondary source is data collected by other people. You might find this data in magazine articles, books or on the internet. You can use these sources to investigate a scientific topic.

Scientific websites, text books, journals, and even dictionaries like this one, are all secondary sources.

It's best to use a variety of sources, to give you an idea of what are so far generally accepted as sensible results for the investigation you're interested in.

Fair tests

Tests are a way of seeing what happens when you try out an idea. Another name for a test is an **experiment.** A test can be anything from a simple measurement to a complicated process that may take days or even years to complete.

To be scientific, a test must be fair. This means that you should change no more than one thing every time you repeat the test (such as the shape of the object you're testing). All the other variables – things that could change – should stay the same.

A fair test to find out if the shape of a piece of modelling clay affects whether it will float

Experiment 1

Modelling clay

Water

Bowl

Experiment 2

* Clay moulded into different shape

✓ Water at same temperature

✓ Same amount of clay

Exploring

Exploring is looking carefully at something that is changing, over a period of time, and recording the changes. Tracking the progress of how something grows or how fast something melts are types of scientific exploration.

You can use exploration to find out how frogspawn develops over a period of 12 weeks.

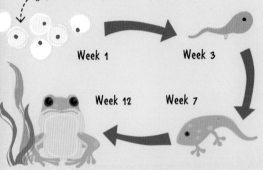

Week 1

Week 3

Week 12

Week 7

Pattern seeking

Pattern seeking is looking at a changing situation where different things can be causing the changes. The changes are recorded to find patterns or connections in the results.

Pattern seeking helps to answer questions which can be difficult to investigate by only changing one factor at a time, such as a person's height or weight.

Pattern seeking to find out whether the length of someone's legs affects how high they can jump

1. Measure the legs of a group of people.

2. Measure how high they can jump.

3. Try to find a pattern in the results.

Classifying

Classifying means grouping things into categories, which are sometimes called classes, based on what they look like or how they behave.

These creepy-crawlies have been separated into different groups, according to how many legs they have.

No legs

 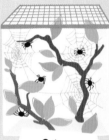

6 legs

8 legs

You can classify things into groups of different sizes, from big ones (such as plants or animals) to very specific ones (such as different types of snail). The more specific the group is, the fewer things will be in it.

Identifying

When you identify something, you decide on which group it belongs to by looking at its features and characteristics.

You can identify which of these metal cans is made of aluminium and which is steel by using a magnet; steel is magnetic and aluminium isn't.

Find out more about: **magnets** (pages 78-79)

Scientific models

A scientific model is a simple model or a picture showing how something works. A model can be created by collecting data about something and looking at it very carefully.

When it would be difficult to carry out experiments and take accurate measurements in the real environment, you can use a model to test out any ideas.

This simple scientific model is a food web. It shows the connections between the foods eaten by animals in a specific habitat.

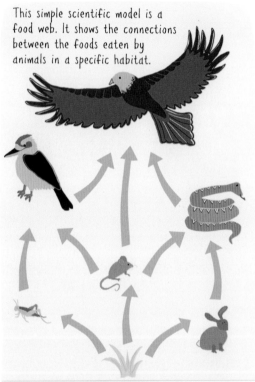

The model shows that removing plants from the habitat will reduce the amount of food available to all the animals in the web.

Your model only needs to show the parts that you want to study and can leave out anything that isn't relevant, otherwise it might become too complicated to understand. If you make a new discovery, you can adjust your model to include it.

Simulations

A simulation is a virtual model made on a computer. Simulations bring scientific models to life, animating how an event might behave and affect its environment over time. Simulations can predict the course of real-life events in nature, such as natural disasters.

Scientists use computer simulations to predict the paths of hurricanes, such as the one below, approaching the coast of Florida, USA.

The colours show the predicted temperatures.

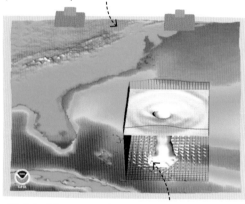

Model of hurricane showing its size

Practical problem solving

Practical problem solving involves finding the solution to a problem by designing and then making something, or connecting objects so that they work together.

You can do tests to answer practical questions, such as: can you light a bulb using just one battery and one wire?

Find out more about: **food webs** (page 43); **habitats** (page 42)

Preparing an investigation

The skills explained on this page will help you prepare a really thorough and accurate scientific investigation.

Observation

Making observations means looking carefully and closely at something. Your observations of the world around you can help you predict what might happen in your investigation.

Once the investigation is underway, you also need your powers of observation to look closely at what is happening, noticing changes and watching out for anything unexpected.

To investigate how long different types of paper planes can stay up in the air, you'll need to observe exactly when they take off and when they land.

Research

Research is reading about a topic to discover new facts about it. Before you start an investigation, it's a good idea to read up about other investigations into the same topic.

Prediction

A prediction is an educated guess about what is going to happen. Your observations, knowledge you already have, and research into the subject can all help you to predict the results of an investigation before you start it.

Planning

Planning is the stage where you decide what you will do to carry out your investigation. For example, you need to choose the method you're going to follow, decide on which equipment to use, and work out the order in which you're going to do things.

Make a balloon rocket

We will need:
A balloon (long would be best)
A long piece of string
A plastic straw
Some tape

Method:
1. Tie one end of the string to something.
2. Put the other end of the string through the straw.
3. Pull the string tight and tie it to another support in the room.
4. Blow up the balloon. Pinch the end and tape the balloon to the straw.
5. Let go and watch the rocket fly.

Find out more about: **scientific investigation** (page 110)

How to do an experiment

If you want to carry out a fair experiment to get an accurate result, you have to follow a step-by-step process.

Identifying the aim

The aim of an experiment is the reason for doing it. Every experiment comes from a question, and your aim should be to find out the answer to your question.

> AIM:
>
> To find out which ball bounces
>
> the highest - a football,
>
> tennis ball, ping pong ball
>
> or rubber ball.

Identifying constants

Constants are the things in an experiment that don't change. They are the objects you always use, or conditions that you want to keep the same every time you carry out the experiment.

> CONSTANTS:
>
> - The height from which each ball will be dropped
> - The surface the balls will be dropped onto

Identifying variables

A variable is the thing that will change each time you carry out the experiment. When you plan an experiment, you have to know what the variables will be. To make the experiment fair, you can only change one thing each time.

VARIABLE: the type of ball

Recording

Recording is making a note of how the experiment was set up and keeping track of the results as they happen. You can record an experiment by:

- making rough sketches and jotting down measurements (for a quick, simple experiment)
- drawing a series of diagrams
- taking photos
- keeping a video diary

This sketch records what happened when an experiment into the bounciness of different balls was carried out.

Football (nearest 0.5cm) - 30, 28.5, 30

Tennis (nearest 0.5cm) - 51, 51.5, 50

Ping pong (nearest 0.5cm) - 58.5, 59, 58

Rubber (nearest 0.5cm) - 66, 66, 66

Taking measurements

A measurement tells you the size of something. Once your experiment is underway, you might need to measure the results, such as how far something has moved, or how much its temperature has changed.

You can use a tape measure or long ruler in an investigation into the bounciness of different balls.

The measurements you take should be accurate and precise so, when you can, take them more than once so you know they're correct. There's more on measuring on pages 116–117.

Writing up results

Writing up is presenting the results of an experiment in a clear way. There are many ways to present results, such as a table, a graph or a chart. There's more on the different ways to write up results on pages 122–125.

The results from the experiment on the opposite page are shown in this table.

Type of ball	Distance (to nearest 0.5cm)			
	Test 1	Test 2	Test 3	Average
Football	30	28.5	30	29.5
Tennis ball	51	51.5	50	51
Ping pong ball	58.5	59	58	58.5
Rubber ball	66	66	66	66

Reaching conclusions

The conclusion is an explanation of your findings. You can reach a conclusion by looking for patterns in your results. The results might fit with what you expected to happen but, if they don't, you might want to do more experiments to find out why not.

CONCLUSION:
- The rubber ball bounced the highest.
- The rubber ball is the same size as the ping pong ball, but the rubber ball is made of solid rubber and squashy, and the ping pong ball is hard and filled with air.
- The other balls are squashy too, but also filled with air.
- Therefore, being both squashy and solid rubber makes the rubber ball bounce higher than the others.

Forming a theory

A theory is a scientific explanation of why something happens, based on the results of a series of experiments. Once you've formed a theory, you can use it to make predictions of what will happen to the thing you've been testing under different circumstances.

Theories aren't definite facts and can be disproved. They might provide good explanations at the time, but are flexible enough to be changed if new evidence comes to light later.

Find out more about: **rulers, tape measures** (page 117); **temperature** (page 50)

Measuring

There are two main measuring systems – the metric and the imperial system. Each uses different units to describe measurements, and these can be marked onto various types of measuring equipment.

Temperature

Temperature is the measurement of how hot or cold something is. The two main systems of measuring temperature are degrees Celsius and Fahrenheit. Temperature is measured in degrees, which can be written as °.

The temperature on a thermometer is shown either on a digital display, or by a coloured liquid moving up its scale.

Volume

Volume is the amount of space something takes up.

Units of volume

Metric:	Imperial:
millilitres (ml)	fluid ounces (fl oz)
centilitres (cl)	pints (pt)
litres (l)	gallons (gal)
cubic centimetres (cc)	cubic inches (in^3)

Measuring jugs and cylinders are see-through containers with measurements marked up the side, used for measuring liquids.

Weight

Weight is to do with how heavy something is. You can find out more about weight on page 72.

Units of weight

Metric:	Imperial:
milligrams (mg)	ounces (oz)
grams (g)	pounds (lb)
kilograms (kg)	stones (st)
tonnes (t)	tons

Examples of equipment used to measure weight

Spring balance – hang an object from the bottom, and a marker on the scale moves down to show the weight.

Balancing scales – put an object on one side, then place weights on the other side until the two sides balance.

Kitchen scales – place a small object in the tray on top and read the scale to find the weight.

Bathroom scales – place a large object on top and read the scale to find the weight.

 Find out more about: **thermometers** (page 94); **units of measurement** (pages 118-121)

Length

Length is the measurement of something from end to end or along its longest side. Length can mean:

- **height** – measured upwards, often from the ground
- **distance** – the length between two objects or places
- **width** – usually measured from side to side
- **depth** – measured downwards from top to bottom, or from front to back

Units of length

Metric:	Imperial:
millimetres (mm)	inches (in)
centimetres (cm)	feet (ft)
metres (m)	yards (yd)
kilometres (km)	miles

Examples of equipment used to measure length

Ruler – a measuring stick used to draw and measure small, straight lines.

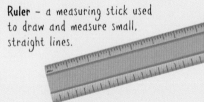

Tape measure – a narrow strip of cloth or metal used to measure longer lengths.

Trundle wheel – a wheel with a handle, which clicks every time it has been pushed one metre.

Time

Time is a measure of how long something takes. The units you use to measure time are based on the movement of the Earth:

- A **year** is the time it takes for the Earth to travel once around the Sun.
- There are 12 **months** in a year.
- A **day** is the time it takes the Earth to spin around once.
- You can divide a day into 24 **hours**.
- Each hour contains 60 **minutes**.
- There are 60 **seconds** in a minute.

Examples of equipment used to measure time

Sandglass – all the sand runs from the top chamber down to the bottom one in a fixed amount of time, such as a minute or an hour.

Stopwatch – a digital timer that you can use to measure short times.

Clock – marks the passing of seconds, minutes and hours. A watch is a small clock worn on the wrist.

Calendar – a chart showing the days and dates for each month of the year.

Units of measurement

A unit of measurement is a way of describing a feature of something by using a quantity. For example, some units describe how big something is, others tell how heavy it is, and others how hot it is. There's more about measuring on pages 116–117.

Measurement system

A measurement system is a set of units of measurement. There are two main systems: imperial and metric. Each one uses a different set of units to describe measurements.

Metric system

The metric system of measuring was introduced in France in the 1790s. It is based on a system of counting in tens, hundreds and thousands, which helps make calculations simpler to do. Scientists worldwide use this system.

Common metric units

Units of length	Written as	Equal to
Millimetre	mm	
Centimetre	cm	10mm
Metre	m	100cm
Kilometre	km	1000m

Units of mass	Written as	Equal to
Milligram	mg	
Gram	g	1000mg
Kilogram	kg	1000g
Tonne	t	1000kg

Units of volume	Written as	Equal to
Millilitre	ml	
Centilitre	cl	10ml
Litre	l	100cl

Imperial system

The imperial system is made up of a set of units that are very old, dating from around the twelfth century. It's used in the UK, along with the metric system. Many other countries still use units based on the imperial system.

Units of measurement in America include pints, feet and pounds. You might have noticed that these are often used to describe food.

Foot-long sandwich   Quarter-pounder burger

Common imperial units

Units of length	Written as	Equal to
Inch	ins or "	
Foot	ft or '	12"
Yard	yd	3'
Mile		1760yd

Units of mass	Written as	Equal to
Ounce	oz	
Pound	lb	16oz
Stone	st	14lb
Ton		160st

Units of volume	Written as	Equal to
Fluid ounce	fl.oz	
Pint	pt	20fl.oz
Gallon	gal	8pt

118 Find out more about: **length** (page 117); **mass** (page 72); **volume** (page 116)

Converting measurements

Converting a measurement means changing it from one type of unit to another.

You can convert a measurement from one unit to another within the same measurement system.

Converting between metric units of length

To change	Into	Do this
millimetres	centimetres	÷10
millimetres	metres	÷1000
centimetres	millimetres	x10
centimetres	metres	÷100
metres	centimetres	x100
metres	kilometres	÷1000
kilometres	metres	x1000

Converting between imperial units of mass

To change	Into	Do this
ounces	pounds	÷16
ounces	stone	÷224
pounds	ounces	x16
pounds	stone	÷14
stone	pounds	x14
stone	tons	÷160
tons	stone	x160

You can also convert measurements from one measurement system to another.

Converting from metric to imperial

To change	Into	Multiply by
centimetres	inches	0.394
metres	yards	1.094
kilometres	miles	0.621
grams	ounces	0.035
kilograms	pounds	2.205
tonnes	tons	0.984
litres	pints	1.76

Converting from imperial to metric

To change	Into	Multiply by
inches	centimetres	2.54
yards	metres	0.914
miles	kilometres	1.609
ounces	grams	28.35
pounds	kilograms	0.454
tons	tonnes	1.016
pints	litres	0.5683

Metric unit names

The names of some metric units give you a clue about their size:

- **Milli...** means one thousandth. One millimetre is one thousandth of a metre.
- **Centi...** means one hundredth. One centilitre is one hundredth of a litre.
- **Kilo...** means one thousand. One kilogram is one thousand grams.

SI units

The units in the modern metric system are known as SI units (short for the French "Système international d'unités"). Before SI units were introduced, there were many measurement systems used worldwide, and even if two countries used the same system, one unit could mean different things in each country. SI units are very precise and are the standard units used in science.

Scales

Many measuring instruments, such as rulers, kitchen scales and measuring jugs have lines called a scale marked on them. Numbers on the lines tell you what the measurements are, and there are often smaller marks in between, to help you measure more accurately.

This ruler shows centimetres along one side. The marks between each centimetre show millimetres.

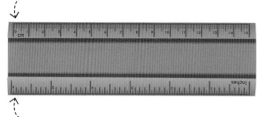

Inches are on the other side. The marks between each inch show eighths and sixteenths of an inch.

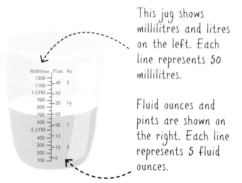

These kitchen scales show kilograms on the outer ring. The lines between each kilogram represent 20g.

Pounds are shown on the inner ring. The lines between each pound represent 1 ounce.

This jug shows millilitres and litres on the left. Each line represents 50 millilitres.

Fluid ounces and pints are shown on the right. Each line represents 5 fluid ounces.

Units of temperature

There are two main measurement systems for temperature: Celsius and Fahrenheit.

Celsius is based on the temperature at which water freezes (0°C) and boils (100°C).

Fahrenheit is based on the temperature of the human body, which was originally measured at 90°F, but has since been changed to 98.6°F.

This thermometer shows Celsius on the left and Fahrenheit on the right. Each line represents 2 degrees.

Converting between units of temperature

To change	Into	Do this
Celsius	Fahrenheit	x9, ÷5, +32
Fahrenheit	Celsius	−32, x5, ÷9

Units of time

Time is divided into a range of units, lasting from the smallest moment up to hundreds of lifetimes.

Unit of time	is equal to
1 minute	60 seconds
1 hour	60 minutes
1 day	24 hours
1 week	7 days
1 year	12 months, or 52 weeks, or 365 days
1 leap year	366 days
1 decade	10 years
1 century	100 years
1 millennium	1000 years

 Find out more about: **measurement** (pages 116-119); **temperature** (page 50); **time** (page 117)

Scale of hardness

The hardness of gemstones and rocks is measured on the Mohs scale. This was named after the German scientist Friedrich Mohs, who invented it in 1812.

Number on Mohs scale	Description	Example stone
1	Very easily scratched with a fingernail	Talc
2	Can be scratched with a fingernail	Gypsum
3	Very easily scratched with a knife	Calcite
4	Easily scratched with a knife	Fluorite
5	Just scratched with a knife	Apatite
6	Can't be scratched with a knife, just scratches glass	Orthoclase
7	Scratches glass easily	Quartz
8	Scratches glass very easily	Topaz
9	Cuts glass	Corundum
10	Cuts glass very easily, scratches corundum	Diamond

Scale of wind force

The Beaufort Scale is a scale for measuring wind force that was developed by British Navy Commander, Sir Francis Beaufort, in 1805. It is a popular way to measure wind speed without using instruments, but by looking at the effects of the wind force.

Beaufort number	Wind speed (kph/mph)	Effects on land
0	under 1	Smoke rises straight up
1	1–5/1–3	Smoke drifts in direction of the wind
2	6–11/4–7	Wind felt on face; leaves rustle
3	12–19/8–12	Leaves and twigs move
4	20–28/13–17	Dust and loose paper lift from ground
5	29–38/18–24	Small trees sway
6	39–49/25–30	Large branches sway; umbrellas hard to use
7	50–61/31–38	Large trees sway; hard to walk against wind
8	62–74/39–46	Twigs break off trees
9	75–88/47–54	Branches break off trees; some damage to buildings
10	89–102/55–63	Trees uprooted; severe damage to buildings
11	103–117/64–72	Widespread damage to trees and buildings
12	118/73 or more	Extreme widespread destruction

Showing your results

How you show the results of a scientific investigation will depend on the type of investigation you're running and the type of information you want to show.

Pictogram

A pictogram uses pictures or symbols to display information. Each symbol represents an amount, and you can use part of a symbol to represent a smaller amount. Use a key to show the amount each symbol represents.

Four bags containing five oranges each were placed around a kitchen. This pictogram shows how many oranges out of each bag had mould growing on them after ten days.

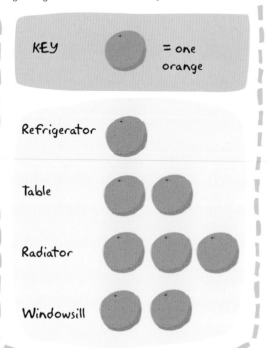

| KEY | ⬤ | = one orange |

Refrigerator
Table
Radiator
Windowsill

Data list

A data list shows each piece of information as you get it. Data like this is **raw data**, which means you need to sort it before you can see anything useful.

This data list shows how many bubbles were produced each time someone blew into a bubble wand.

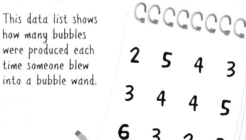

2 5 4 3
3 4 4 5
6 3 2 3

Tally chart

You can collect and sort data on a tally chart by drawing a line called a tally to show each item you count. Mark the fifth in each group as a line across, like a gate. This makes it easier to add them. By adding the tallies in each row, you can see the **frequency** – the number of times the same piece of information occurs.

This tally chart shows how many baby teeth are lost by a class of 7-8 year olds over 6 months.

Month	Tally	Frequency
January	I	1
February	III	3
March		0
April	II	2
May	IIII	5
June	IIII	4

Find out more about: **data** (page 110);
scientific investigation (pages 110-112)

Table

A table is a way of showing information by setting it out into rows (going across) and columns (going down). Presenting your results in a table is a good way of comparing the results of different tests within an investigation.

This table shows the results of a test to see which brand of paper towel sucks up the most water in 30 seconds.

Brand of paper towel	Volume of water soaked up (ml)		
	Test 1	Test 2	Average
Kleenup	29	28	28.5
Absorbit	30	29	29.5
Drinkin	28	28	28

Grouping data

Sometimes it can help you understand information if you put the data into groups. You can do this by arranging the numbers on a data list into groups then finding the frequency for each group. This helps you see which group has the most entries.

This data list shows how many stars a group of 25 children could count from outside their house at the same time on the same night.

84	93	112	49	68
65	96	22	104	79
35	61	40	77	83
52	29	72	51	92
38	59	67	42	86

Grouping the data shows that the most common number of stars seen in the sky that night were between 61 and 80.

Number of stars	Tally	Frequency
0-20		0
21-40	IIII	5
41-60	IIII	5
61-80	IIII II	7
81-100	IIII I	6
101-120	II	2

Pie chart

A pie chart is a circle split into sections to show information. The whole circle represents 100% of something and each section stands for a percentage of the whole. The size of the section shows how big the percentage is.

These pie charts show the grades achieved by a class of students for two tests. They took one test after sleeping for 8 hours the night before, then took the other one having slept only 6 hours.

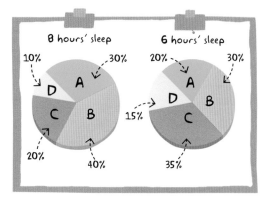

Pie charts are good for showing information at a glance when there are no more than six sections – otherwise, the chart would be too busy to understand. They're not very useful when the values of each section are similar because it is difficult to see the differences between slice sizes.

Bar charts

A bar chart is a way of comparing the results of separate tests within one investigation, using bars to represent each test. The height of each bar shows the value of the results of each test.

This bar chart shows the results of an experiment to test the life of different brands of batteries.

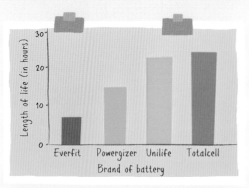

Histograms

Histograms are similar to bar charts but, in a bar chart, all of the bars are the same width and only the height matters. In a histogram, it's the area, not the height, that matters. You use histograms when you want to show results for groups of different sizes.

This histogram shows the ages of the elephants within a herd.

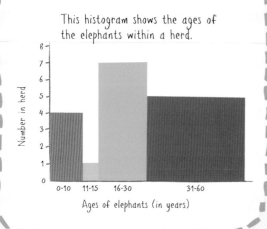

Venn diagrams

A Venn diagram uses overlapping circles to show relationships between sets of information. The things within each circle have a feature in common. Things that are in both circles, where they overlap, have both features.

This Venn diagram shows the results of an exploration into the species living in different types of compost.

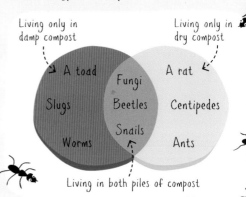

Line graphs

Line graphs show the relationship between one quantity and another by representing information as points on a graph, joined together to make a line. They're often used to show how something changes over time.

This line graph shows how the number of times a balloon is rubbed against a woollen jumper affects how long it will stick to a wall.

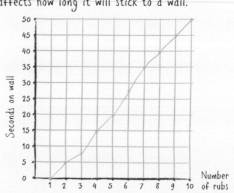

Scatter diagrams

A scatter diagram lets you show lots of information at the same time to see if there's any connection between them. Sometimes there isn't but, when there is, then the pattern of the dots you draw on the graph might form a straight line if you connect them.

This scatter diagram shows how far three types of paper planes flew at different windspeeds.

◆ Plane 1
■ Plane 2
▲ Plane 3

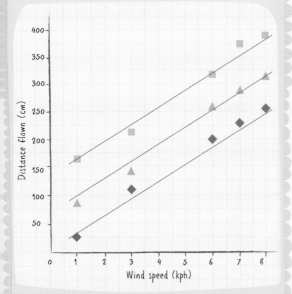

Distance flown (cm) / Wind speed (kph)

You can draw straight lines through most of the points for each plane. The lines slope at a similar angle, showing that the distance travelled by each plane increased by roughly the same amount as the wind speed increased.

Often in a scatter diagram, you can only connect some of the dots in a straight line, and others might be just above or below the line.

Carroll diagrams

A Carroll diagram is a chart that helps you to sort information into categories. To use one, you need to decide which box each item should go into.

Chopping board

Rubber duck

Raincoat

Grater

Ginger biscuit

Pencil case

Teddy bear

Sponge

Sieve

Umbrella

Magazine

Garden gnome

The Carroll diagram below sorts out the items above into groups depending on whether they're waterproof, flexible, or both.

	Waterproof	Not waterproof
Flexible	Pencil case Raincoat Umbrella	Magazine Sponge Teddy bear
Not flexible	Garden gnome Chopping board Rubber duck	Sieve Grater Ginger biscuit

Famous scientists

The people on these pages have made important scientific discoveries that shaped the way we look at the world today.

Ibn al-Haytham (965-1038)

This early scientist was born in what is now Iraq. He was one of the first people to use the scientific method. His investigations into the behaviour of light explained how light is related to seeing, colour and shadows.

Al-Haytham experimented with light using lamps and candles.

Archimedes (287-212BC)

This Ancient Greek scientist and mathematician is famous for discovering that a floating object displaces its own weight in water. He also invented a variety of machines, including pulleys and a screw-shaped pumping device.

Legend has it that Archimedes discovered displacement when getting into the bath. He then jumped out and ran around yelling "Eureka!", which means "I found it!".

Eureka!

Anders Celsius (1701-1744)

The Celsius temperature scale is named after its Swedish inventor. Celsius invented the first temperature scale that was divided into 100 degree units.

Nicolaus Copernicus (1473-1543)

This Polish astronomer put forward the idea that the planets move around the Sun. Before this, it was thought that the Sun and planets moved around the Earth.

Copernicus studied lunar eclipses to find out how the Earth moves.

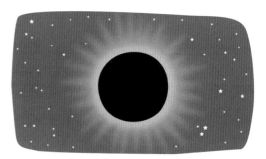

Albert Einstein (1879-1955)

Einstein was one of the most famous scientists who ever lived. He came up with many important ideas about light, gravity, mass and energy.

Einstein had many ideas about how energy and mass are related, which he expressed using letters, symbols and numbers.

$$E = MC^2$$

Find out more about: **displacement** (page 81); **gravity** (pages 72-73); **mass** (page 72)

Daniel Gabriel Fahrenheit (1686-1736)

This Polish-born scientist invented the mercury thermometer and came up with the Fahrenheit temperature scale. He based his scale on the temperature of the human body, which was originally measured at 90°F, but is now 98.6°F.

Benjamin Franklin (1706-1790)

Franklin was an American politician and scientist who invented a whole list of useful devices, such as bifocal spectacles, the speedometer, and the lightning rod. He is most famous for his experiments to prove that lightning is a form of electricity.

Franklin noted that a key would spark if it was tied to the string of a kite flying in a thunderstorm.

Galileo Galilei (1564-1642)

This Italian astronomer developed a telescope through which he saw planets and moons. He also made important discoveries about motion and machines.

Galileo discovered the planet Jupiter's four largest moons through his telescope.

William Gilbert (1544-1603)

Gilbert was a doctor to Queen Elizabeth I of England. He was the first person to study magnetism using the scientific method. He explained the difference between magnetism and static, and put forward the idea that the Earth itself is magnetic.

Gilbert was the first person to explore the similarity between a magnet and the Earth.

William Harvey (1578-1657)

Harvey was a doctor to kings James I and Charles I of England. He discovered how blood circulates through the body, and was also the first to suggest that humans and other mammals reproduced by the fertilization of an egg by sperm.

Stephen Hawking (1942-)

This English physicist has made important investigations into the behaviour of black holes and how the universe was made.

Robert Hooke (1635-1703)

This English scientist discovered the relationship between elasticity and force. He also discovered plant cells and was the first person to use the word "cell".

Find out more about: **elasticity** (page 80)

James Joule (1818-1889)

The joule, a unit of measurement of work and heat, is named after this English scientist who made important investigations into these areas.

Antoine Lavoisier (1743-1794)

This French scientist and lawyer carried out investigations into a gas which he named oxygen. He explained how oxygen is used in respiration, how it is needed for things to burn, how it rusts metals and how it is a part of water.

Lavoisier discovered that a burning candle goes out when it runs out of oxygen.

Antony van Leeuwenhoek (1632-1723)

Known as "the father of microscopy", this Dutch scientist created over 400 different types of microscope and used his inventions to discover bacteria, blood cells and sperm cells.

Leeuwenhoek discovered blobs of bacteria when examining lake water through one of his microscopes.

Carl Linnaeus (1707-1778)

Linnaeus was a Swedish scientist and doctor. He created a system for grouping living things into different categories depending on what they look like or how they behave.

This is how Linnaeus would classify himself (a human) using his system.

Kingdom:	Animalia
Phylum:	Chordata
Class:	Mammalia
Order:	Primates
Family:	Hominidae
Genus:	Homo
Species:	Homo sapiens

Isaac Newton (1642-1727)

This English scientist discovered gravity and made important investigations into motion. He also discovered that light is made up of different colours, and built the first telescope that used curved mirrors.

Legend has it that Newton started thinking about gravity when an apple fell on his head as he sat under a tree.

Georg Ohm (1787-1854)

This German scientist carried out investigations into electricity and the relationship between voltage and current. He also investigated how we hear sounds.

Blaise Pascal (1623-1662)

Pressure is measured in units called pascals, which are named after this French scientist. Pascal's experiments greatly increased knowledge of how air and water react to pressure.

Pressure gauge

Pascal sent his friends and family up mountains with air pressure gauges to measure the air pressure at different heights.

Louis Pasteur (1822-1895)

This French scientist was the first to show that disease and rotting were caused by bacteria. He invented pasteurization – a way of making food last longer by killing bacteria with heat, and made vaccines to protect people and animals against a variety of diseases.

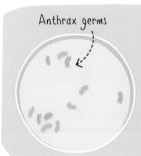

Anthrax germs

Pasteur discovered that animals could be protected against a deadly disease called anthrax by being injected with heated anthrax germs.

Joseph Priestley (1733-1804)

Priestley was an English scientist who discovered that air was made up of different gases. He also invented fizzy drinks.

Wilhelm Röntgen (1845-1923)

This German scientist discovered x-rays when he was studying what happened when an electric current passed through a gas at extremely low pressure.

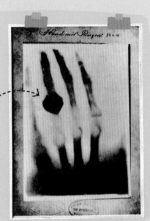

This is the first ever x-ray image taken. It shows Röntgen's wife's hand, with a wedding ring around her finger.

Andreas Vesalius (1514-1564)

Vesalius was a Belgian doctor whose studies and drawings of the different parts of the human body helped to explain how the body works.

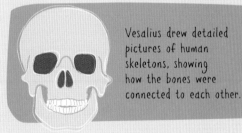

Vesalius drew detailed pictures of human skeletons, showing how the bones were connected to each other.

Alessandro Volta (1745-1827)

The volt, a unit of measurement of electric potential, is named after this Italian scientist who made the first ever electric battery.

Find out more about: **bacteria** (page 40); **electric potential** see **voltage** (page 87)

Index

Acknowledgements

Every effort has been made to trace the copyright holders of the material in this book. If any rights have been omitted, the publishers offer to rectify this in any future edition, following notification.

(l=left, r=right, t=top, m=middle, b=bottom)
20 © WizData,inc./Alamy; 40 © JAMES CAVALLINI/SCIENCE PHOTO LIBRARY; 52 © VEER.com; 79 © Phil Degginger/Alamy; 90 © VEER.com; 93 © VEER.com; 97 © Archie George Hill; 100 (ml) © NASA/ESA/OU/ICL/STSI/U.Va/WFC3 SOC (et al); 100 (bml) © NASA/ESA/STScl/AURA; 100 (bl) © NASA/ESA/STScl/CFHT/NOAO; 100 (tr) © NASA/JPL-Caltech; 101 (tl) © Digital Vision; 101 (tr) © N.Smith, J.A. Morse (U.Colorado) et al., NASA; 101 (br) © DETLEV VAN RAVENSWAAY/SCIENCE PHOTO LIBRARY; 106 (tr) © NASA/JPL; 107 (bl) © NASA; 107 (br) © Fred Espenak/NASA's Goddard Space Flight Center; 109 (tr) © NASA; 112 © GFDL/NOAA; 129 © SSPL via Getty Images

Additional designs by Karen Tomlins
and Candice Whatmore